Vegetarian Times **LOW-FAT** & *Fast*

Mexican

Vegetarian Times
Low-Fat & *Fast*
Mexican

From the editors of
Vegetarian Times magazine

Macmillan • USA

MACMILLAN

A Simon & Schuster Macmillan Company
1633 Broadway
New York, NY 10019-6785

Macmillan Publishing books may be purchased for business or sales promotional use. For information please write: Special Markets Department, Macmillan Publishing USA, 1633 Broadway, New York, NY 10019.

Library of Congress Cataloging-in-Publication Data

Vegetarian times low-fat & fast Mexican cookbook /by the editors of Vegetarian times.
    p. cm.
    Includes index.
    ISBN 0-02-862149-2 (alk. paper)
    1. Vegetarian cookery.   2. Cookery, Mexican   3. Low-fat diet—
    recipes.   4. Quick and easy cookery.   I. Vegetarian times.
    TX837.V4277   1998
    641.5'636—dc21   97-38970
                                                  CIP

Manufactured in the United States of America

10 9 8 7 6 5 4 3 2 1

Book design by Amy Peppler Adams, designLab, Seattle

Contents

Acknowledgments

The editors of *Vegetarian Times* would like to thank Jay Solomon for his continued devotion, expertise, and professionalism in the development of these wonderful recipes. Jay's talent extends beyond the kitchen; his writing is elegant, witty, and always on the money.

Thanks also to Karin Horgan Sullivan, former senior editor of *Vegetarian Times*, and to Terry Christofferson, assistant editor, for putting this manuscript together for me. It couldn't have been in more capable hands, and there are no two people I'd trust more to undertake such a job.

—Carol Wiley Lorente,
Special Projects Editor,
Vegetarian Times

Introduction

Welcome to the *Vegetarian Times Low-Fat & Fast Mexican* cookbook, fourth in the series of cookbooks that are guaranteed to satisfy your need for healthful, meatless cooking and your desire to get food on the table fast.

Vegetarian Times has been the authority on meatless cooking and the vegetarian lifestyle since 1974. We first undertook the Low-Fat & Fast cookbook series in 1996 after the resounding success of our magazine *Low-Fat & Fast*. Based on our popular magazine column, it was named the Best Newsstand Introduction of the year. We knew the demand for low-fat recipes simply was not going to wane anytime soon.

And it hasn't. More than ever, Americans recognize that they need to eat a diet low in fat and high in complex carbohydrates to help prevent heart disease, obesity, diabetes, and the other illnesses that ravage our society.

But low-fat meals aren't enough. More and more Americans want meatless meals, they want them to taste good, and they want them quickly. That's what the Low-Fat & Fast cookbook series is all about. Each volume in the series offers 150 to 200 recipes—appetizers and snacks, soups, salads, main dishes, side dishes, and desserts. And whether you're a vegetarian for reasons of health, animal rights, environment, or religion, you'll find plenty to like here. All of the recipes are low in fat and call for few if any animal products (and no meat, fish, or poultry whatsoever).

HOW TO USE THIS COOKBOOK

The idea for a book of Mexican recipes fits in seamlessly with the guidelines for a good diet: Mexican cuisine features meals based on complex carbohydrates, especially legumes, with lots of vegetables too. Our recipes fit in with these guiding principles. The recipe developer for this volume is Jay Solomon, a chef and the author of twelve cookbooks. Jay is also a well-traveled culinary adventurer, and the influence of his globe-trotting and poblano peppers; nopales and nopalitos; and masa harina can be found in some supermarkets, natural food stores, and in Mexican markets. Textured vegetable protein (TVP), rice milk, and seitan are available in natural food stores. Bok choy and shiitake mushrooms can be found at well-stocked supermarkets and Asian grocery stores.

We think you'll find *Vegetarian Times Low-Fat & Fast Mexican* an invaluable guide to cooking fast, healthful, vegetarian meals. Happy cooking.

Introduction

Welcome to the *Vegetarian Times Low-Fat & Fast Mexican* cookbook, fourth in the series of cookbooks that are guaranteed to satisfy your need for healthful, meatless cooking and your desire to get food on the table fast.

Vegetarian Times has been the authority on meatless cooking and the vegetarian lifestyle since 1974. We first undertook the Low-Fat & Fast cookbook series in 1996 after the resounding success of our magazine *Low-Fat & Fast*. Based on our popular magazine column, it was named the Best Newsstand Introduction of the year. We knew the demand for low-fat recipes simply was not going to wane anytime soon.

And it hasn't. More than ever, Americans recognize that they need to eat a diet low in fat and high in complex carbohydrates to help prevent heart disease, obesity, diabetes, and the other illnesses that ravage our society.

But low-fat meals aren't enough. More and more Americans want meatless meals, they want them to taste good, and they want them quickly. That's what the Low-Fat & Fast cookbook series is all about. Each volume in the series offers 150 to 200 recipes—appetizers and snacks, soups, salads, main dishes, side dishes, and desserts. And whether you're a vegetarian for reasons of health, animal rights, environment, or religion, you'll find plenty to like here. All of the recipes are low in fat and call for few if any animal products (and no meat, fish, or poultry whatsoever).

HOW TO USE THIS COOKBOOK

The idea for a book of Mexican recipes fits in seamlessly with the guidelines for a good diet: Mexican cuisine features meals based on complex carbohydrates, especially legumes, with lots of vegetables too. Our recipes fit in with these guiding principles. The recipe developer for this volume is Jay Solomon, a chef and the author of twelve cookbooks. Jay is also a well-traveled culinary adventurer, and the influence of his globe-trotting shows up in many dishes here. Besides recipes based solely on traditionally Mexican ingredients, you'll also find some with overtones from other cultures—Poblano-Cilantro Hummus (page 17), for example, and Asian Burritos with Stir-Fried Vegetables (page 96).

The recipes Jay has created are simple to prepare. We are not kidding when we say that if you can boil water, chop vegetables, and stir, you can cook every recipe in this book! We would encourage you to do a couple of things before you begin cooking, however. First, read "How to Cook Low-Fat" (below) and "About Our Recipes" (page ix).

HOW TO COOK LOW-FAT

Eating a low-fat diet—and cooking low-fat meals—isn't as difficult as you might think. Our advice has always been to base your meals and snacks on whole grains, beans, fruits, and vegetables; they're naturally low in fat and calories, and they contain all of the vitamins, minerals, and fiber you need.

Most of the recipes in this cookbook take around 30 minutes or less to prepare. But getting your own favorite meals on the table also can be easier when you know a few tricks. Most of it boils down to planning and completing tasks as the food cooks. Here are some tips for quick cooking:

- Set out all ingredients and utensils you'll need before you begin cooking, and mentally organize the preparation so you can "dovetail" steps. For example, while the rice is cooking, chop the garlic and onion for the sauce. (We have written the recipes so this will happen.)

- Organize and equip your kitchen to your advantage. Keep frequently used utensils, such as wooden spoons, rubber scrapers, spatulas, and whisks in a container or drawer next to the stove; keep pots, pans, mixing bowls, and measuring cups nearby. And return these items to the same places so you won't have to hunt for them next time.

- Wholesome, nutritious foods do come in convenient, prepared forms—use them! Frozen vegetables, canned beans, bagged, cut-up, and shredded produce, quick-cooking rice, canned vegetable broths, and other prepared foods are wholesome and of good quality and save time. Don't forget the supermarket salad bar as a source for cut-up vegetables, and the canned food aisle for prepared garlic, roasted red peppers, etc.

➤ There are simple ways to speed the actual heating and cooking of foods. Smaller and thinner cuts of vegetables cook more quickly than thick ones. Wide-diameter skillets and pots speed up heating and simmering. Also, when you need to boil water, start with hot tap water to speed things along. (Every little bit helps!)

ABOUT OUR RECIPES

After each recipe, we provide nutritional information that lists the amount of calories, protein, fat, carbohydrates, cholesterol, sodium, and fiber per serving. When a choice of ingredients is given (as in "skim milk or soy milk"), the analysis reflects the first ingredient listed (skim milk). When there is a range of servings (as in "1 to 2 tablespoons olive oil"), the analysis reflects the first number listed (1 tablespoon). When an ingredient is listed as optional, it is not included in the nutritional analysis.

We do not list the percentage of calories from fat per serving because we believe it is misleading. The percent of fat in a given recipe is less important than the percent of fat eaten in an entire day. The bulk of research indicates that fat intake must be less than 25 percent of calories to prevent disease and to promote health. So if you eat 2,000 calories per day, you can eat 55 grams of fat per day and maintain a diet that obtains 25 percent of calories from fat.

Where appropriate, we also give variations and helpful hints after recipes.

ABOUT THE INGREDIENTS

For the most part, our recipes call for familiar ingredients that are easy to find in supermarkets or natural food stores. Some of our recipes use ingredients that are a bit more unusual. However, even these ingredients can often be found in your local stores. (Of course, if you have a Mexican grocery in your community, you're home free.) Keep in mind that this cookbook was developed and tested in a home kitchen much like yours, located in a small community in upstate New York. All of the ingredients we call for in this book were readily available, so it is likely they'll be available where you live too.

For instance, jicama, jalapeños (both fresh and jarred), tomatillos, commercial taco seasoning in packets, hominy corn (canned or frozen), and corn spirals are readily available in most large supermarkets and natural food stores. Other ingredients, such as chayote; chitpotle, habanero, ancho, and poblano peppers; nopales and nopalitos; and masa harina can be found in some supermarkets, natural food stores, and in Mexican markets. Textured vegetable protein (TVP), rice milk, and seitan are available in natural food stores. Bok choy and shiitake mushrooms can be found at well-stocked supermarkets and Asian grocery stores.

We think you'll find *Vegetarian Times Low-Fat & Fast Mexican* an invaluable guide to cooking fast, healthful, vegetarian meals. Happy cooking.

CHAPTER 1

Appetizers

Red Chili Paste

This potent chili sauce can be blended into soups and stews or served with spicy burritos, tostadas, or quesadillas. Red chili pastes, or sauces, are used to flavor a variety of Mexican dishes, much like garlicky pesto is used in Italian cuisine.

3 to 4 dried Mexican chilies (such as pasilla, ancho, or guajillo)
1 cup simmering water
¼ cup diced yellow onion
1 large clove garlic, chopped
½ teaspoon salt
¼ teaspoon freshly ground black pepper
⅛ teaspoon ground cloves

Remove the stems and seeds from the chilies. Heat a large ungreased skillet over medium heat, then add the chilies and cook, stirring, until lightly toasted, about 2 minutes. Shake the pan and turn the chilies a few times as they cook. Remove from the heat and cover the chilies with the water. Place a lid or plate over the chilies to keep them from floating. Let soak until soft, 15 to 20 minutes. Drain and reserve ½ cup of the soaking liquid.

Add the chilies, reserved soaking liquid, onion, garlic, and seasonings to a blender or food processor fitted with a steel blade and process until smooth, about 5 seconds. Scrape the pureed mixture into a small bowl.

Add the chili paste to soups, chili, stews, burritos, or serve as a barbecue sauce. (Use it in moderation though; a little goes a long way.) Refrigerate the remaining paste for later.

**Makes ¾ cup
(36 teaspoons)**

Per teaspoon:
1 Calorie; 0 Protein; 0 Fat;
0 Carbohydrates; 0 Cholesterol;
32mg Sodium; 0 Fiber

Ancho Chili–Sun-Dried Tomato Paste

*This smooth-textured paste has a deep, robust flavor and musky heat.
For an intriguing change of pace, spread it over a burrito or quesadilla
along with traditional salsa or salsa verde.*

2 ancho chilies
2 cups simmering water
½ cup sun-dried tomatoes
    (not oil-packed)
One 14-ounce can stewed
    tomatoes, partially drained
⅓ cup diced yellow onion
1 large clove garlic, chopped
1 teaspoon dried oregano
½ teaspoon salt
½ teaspoon freshly ground
    black pepper

Remove the stems and seeds from the chilies. Place a large ungreased skillet over medium heat and add the chilies. Cook, stirring, until lightly toasted, about 2 minutes. Shake the pan and turn the chilies a few times as they cook. Remove from the heat and cover the chilies with the simmering water. Stir in the sun-dried tomatoes and place a lid or plate over the chilies and tomatoes to keep them from floating. Let soak until soft, about 15 minutes.

Add the chilies, sun-dried tomatoes, stewed tomatoes, onion, garlic, oregano, salt, and pepper to a medium saucepan. Bring to a simmer and cook over medium-high heat, stirring, for 5 minutes. Transfer the mixture to a blender or food processor fitted with a steel blade and process until smooth, about 5 seconds. Pour (or scrape) the sauce into a serving bowl.

Serve the sauce warm or cold with burritos, quesadillas, or tostadas.

Makes 2 cups
(32 tablespoons)

Per tablespoon:
8 Calories; 0 Protein; 0 Fat;
2g Carbohydrates; 0 Cholesterol;
96mg Sodium; 0 Fiber

Easy Taco Sauce

Although there are scores of taco sauces on the market, it is easy to cook up a homemade version. Serve this versatile sauce with tacos, tostadas, burritos, enchiladas, and other tortilla dishes.

1 tablespoon canola oil
1 small yellow onion, finely
  chopped
2 cloves garlic, minced
One 6-ounce can tomato paste
2 cups water
1 to 3 teaspoons chopped
  pickled jalapeños
1½ teaspoons red wine vinegar
1 teaspoon dried oregano
½ teaspoon ground cumin
½ teaspoon salt
½ teaspoon freshly ground
  black pepper
1 teaspoon sugar

In a medium saucepan, heat the oil over medium heat. Add the onion and garlic and cook, stirring, until the onion is translucent, about 3 minutes. Stir in the remaining ingredients. Stir until tomato paste and water are completely blended, about 30 seconds.

Increase heat to medium-high and bring the sauce to a simmer, stirring frequently.

Reduce the heat to low and cook, uncovered, stirring occasionally, until thickened, 12 to 15 minutes. Remove the sauce from the heat and transfer to serving bowl. Serve the sauce with tacos, burritos, quesadillas, or tostadas.

**Makes 2½ cups
(40 tablespoons)**

Per tablespoon:
9 Calories; 0 Protein; 0 Fat;
1g Carbohydrates; 0 Cholesterol;
33mg Sodium; 0 Fiber

Tomatillo-Chipotle Sauce

Tomatillos have a mildly tart flavor, somewhere between lime and mild vinegar. Here they team up with smoky chipotle chilies. Serve the sauce with tomato-based dishes and burritos.

1 tablespoon canola oil
1 small yellow onion, diced
2 cloves garlic, minced
One 12-ounce can whole
   tomatillos, drained
¾ cup vegetable stock
1 or 2 canned chipotle chilies,
   seeded and minced
½ teaspoon ground cumin
½ teaspoon salt
½ teaspoon freshly ground
   black pepper
2 tablespoons chopped cilantro

In a medium saucepan, heat the oil over medium-high heat. Add the onion and garlic and cook, stirring, until tender, 3 to 4 minutes. Add the tomatillos, vegetable stock, chipotles, cumin, salt, and pepper and bring to a simmer. Cook, stirring, about 7 minutes.

Transfer the mixture to a blender or food processor fitted with a steel blade and process until smooth, about 5 seconds. Return to the pan and reduce heat to medium-low. Cook, stirring, for about 10 minutes. Stir in the cilantro. Serve the sauce with tortilla dishes or as a dip. Refrigerate any leftover sauce for later use.

**Makes 1½ cups
(Six ¼-cup servings)**

Per serving:
48 Calories; 0 Protein; 4g Fat;
4g Carbohydrates; 0 Cholesterol;
82mg Sodium; 0 Fiber

Versatile Tomato Salsa

Although there are scores of commercial salsas on the market, it is easy and rewarding to make your own. This version is heightened with lime, cilantro, and the indispensable jalapeño peppers.

2 ripe tomatoes, diced
1 green bell pepper, seeded
   and diced
1 medium yellow onion, diced
2 cloves garlic, minced
1 to 2 tablespoons minced
   pickled jalapeños
2 tablespoons chopped cilantro
Juice of 1 lime
2 teaspoons dried oregano
1 teaspoon ground cumin
½ teaspoon salt
½ teaspoon cayenne pepper
One 16-ounce can crushed
   tomatoes

In a large mixing bowl, mix together all of the ingredients. Place three-quarters of the mixture in a blender or food processor fitted with a steel blade and process for 5 seconds, creating a chunky vegetable mash.

Return the mashed vegetables to the bowl and mix together. Chill the salsa for 15 minutes to allow the flavors to meld. Serve the salsa with warm flour tortillas or as a side to burritos or quesadillas.

Makes 4 cups
(Sixteen ¼-cup servings)

Per serving:
10 Calories, 0 Protein; 0 Fat;
2g Carbohydrates; 0 Cholesterol;
89mg Sodium; 0 Fiber

Roasted Pepper Salsa

Roasted chili peppers bring a smoky flavor to this robust and chunky salsa.

**2 poblano or New Mexico
  chilies, cored and seeded**
2 ripe tomatoes, diced
1 medium yellow onion, diced
2 cloves garlic, minced
**2 to 3 tablespoons chopped
  cilantro**
Juice of 1 lime
2 teaspoons dried oregano
1 teaspoon ground cumin
½ teaspoon salt
½ teaspoon cayenne pepper
**One 16 ounce can crushed
  tomatoes**

Preheat the broiler.

Arrange the chilies on a baking sheet. Broil, turning once, until the skins are slightly charred all over, 4 to 5 minutes on each side. Remove from the heat and let cool for a few minutes. With a butter knife (or your hands—wear rubber gloves to protect your skin), peel off the charred skin and discard. Finely chop the flesh.

In a large mixing bowl, blend the roasted chilies together with the remaining ingredients. Place three-quarters of the mixture in a blender or food processor fitted with a steel blade and process, creating a chunky vegetable mash, about 5 seconds. Return the mashed vegetables to the bowl and blend together again.

Chill the salsa for 15 minutes to allow the flavors to meld. Serve with warm flour tortillas or as a condiment with burritos, quesadillas, or tacos.

**Makes 4 cups
(Sixteen ¼-cup servings)**

Per serving:
9 Calories; 0 Protein; 0 Fat;
2g Carbohydrates; 0 Cholesterol;
104mg Sodium; 1g Fiber

Fiesta Jicama and Corn Salsa

*The crisp texture of jicama makes it a
favorite ingredient for salsas and salads.*

2 tomatoes, chopped
1 cup peeled and diced jicama
1 cup cooked corn kernels
1 small yellow onion, chopped
2 whole scallions, trimmed and
    chopped
2 tablespoons chopped cilantro
2 tablespoons chopped fresh
    parsley
2 to 3 teaspoons pickled
    jalapeños, minced
Juice of ½ lime
½ teaspoon salt
¼ teaspoon cayenne pepper
1½ tablespoons tomato paste
¼ cup water

In a medium mixing bowl, blend
together all of the ingredients.
Chill for 15 minutes to allow the
flavors to meld. Serve the salsa
with burritos, quesadillas, or
tostadas.

**Makes 2 cups
(Eight ¼-cup servings)**

Per serving:
39 Calories; 1g Protein; 0 Fat;
9g Carbohydrates; 0 Cholesterol;
217mg Sodium; 2g Fiber

Sun-Dried Tomato Salsa

*Balsamic vinegar and sun-dried tomatoes
add acidic nuance to this tempting salsa.*

½ cup sun-dried tomatoes
    (not oil-packed)
1 tomato, diced
¼ cup diced red onion
2 whole scallions, trimmed
    and chopped
2 tablespoons chopped cilantro
1 clove garlic, minced
1 tablespoon balsamic vinegar
1 tablespoon canola oil
½ teaspoon salt
½ teaspoon freshly ground
    black pepper

In a small saucepan, bring 3 cups of water to a boil. Place the sun-dried tomatoes in the boiling water and cook over medium-low heat until tender, about 3 minutes. Drain the tomatoes, reserving 1 to 2 tablespoons of the liquid. Coarsely chop the tomatoes.

Add the sun-dried tomatoes and reserved liquid along with the remaining ingredients to a blender or food processor fitted with a steel blade and process for 3 to 4 seconds. Transfer to a small bowl and serve with quesadillas, burritos, or tacos. There should be enough for 6 quesadillas or 4 burritos.

**Makes 1½ cups
(Six ¼-cup servings)**

Per serving:
40 Calories; 1g Protein; 2g Fat;
4g Carbohydrates; 0 Cholesterol;
291mg Sodium; 1g Fiber

Salsa Verde

This smooth-textured sauce is prepared with tomatillos, those slightly sour, green tomato–like fruits cloaked in paper husks. (Salsa verde means "green sauce.") This shortcut version makes use of canned tomatillos.

1 tablespoon canola oil
1 small yellow onion, diced
2 cloves garlic, minced
One 12-ounce can whole
    tomatillos, drained
¾ cup vegetable stock
1 tablespoon pickled jalapeños
½ teaspoon salt
½ teaspoon freshly ground
    black pepper
2 tablespoons chopped cilantro

In a medium saucepan, heat the oil over medium-high heat. Add the onion and garlic and cook, stirring, until tender, 3 to 4 minutes. Add the tomatillos, vegetable stock, jalapeños, salt, and black pepper, and bring to a simmer. Cook, stirring frequently, about 7 minutes.

Transfer the mixture to a blender or food processor fitted with a steel blade and process until smooth, about 5 seconds. Reduce heat to medium-low and return mixture to the pan. Cook, stirring frequently, about 10 minutes. Stir in the cilantro. Serve the sauce with filled tortilla dishes. Refrigerate any leftover sauce for later use.

**Makes 1½ cups
(24 tablespoons)**

Per tablespoon:
12 Calories; 0 Protein; 0 Fat;
1g Carbohydrates; 0 Cholesterol;
85mg Sodium; 0 Fiber

Avocado-Corn Salsa

*Avocados lend a rich, decadent flavor to
this simple salsa of tomatoes and corn.*

**2 ripe avocados, peeled, pitted,
and diced (see Helpful
Hints)**
2 plum tomatoes, diced
**1 cup corn kernels (canned or
fresh)**
1 large clove garlic, minced
**2 whole scallions, trimmed
and chopped**
**1 tablespoon pickled jalapeños,
minced**
2 tablespoons chopped cilantro
Juice of 1 lime
½ teaspoon ground cumin
½ teaspoon salt
**½ teaspoon freshly ground
black pepper**

Place all of the ingredients in a
medium mixing bowl and gently
toss together, being careful not to
mash the avocado pieces. Transfer
to a serving bowl and serve as a
condiment with burritos, tostadas,
or quesadillas. The salsa can also
be served as a chunky dip.

**Makes about 2 cups
(Eight ¼-cup servings)**

Helpful Hints

*To determine the degree of ripeness
of an avocado, hold the fruit in the
base of your hand and press on the
skin with the thumb of the hand
you're holding the avocado with; it
should give a little. Green, unripe
avocados will ripen in a few days
if stored at room temperature. To
keep the inside of an avocado from
turning dark, sprinkle with a little
lime or lemon juice.*

Per serving:
108 Calories; 4g Protein; 8g Fat;
12g Carbohydrates; 0 Cholesterol;
232mg Sodium; 4g Fiber

Chili Rajas

Chili rajas *refers to strips of roasted peppers (*rajas *means "splinters").*
The chilies are blended into a garnish or filling for tostadas,
burritos, pilafs, or quesadillas.

4 poblano chilies, cored
  and seeded
2 teaspoons canola oil
1 small yellow onion, diced
2 cloves garlic, minced
1 tomato, diced
½ teaspoon dried oregano
½ teaspoon salt

Roast the chilies by placing them over an open flame or beneath a broiler for 4 to 6 minutes on each side until the skin is charred all over. Remove the chilies from the heat and let cool for a few minutes. With a butter knife (or your hands—wear rubber gloves to protect your skin), scrape the charred skin from the flesh and discard. Cut the chilies into ¼-inch-wide strips.

In a large skillet, heat the oil over medium-high heat. Add the onion and garlic and cook, stirring, until the onion is translucent, about 4 minutes. Add the chili strips, tomato, oregano, and salt and cook, stirring, over medium heat until the tomato becomes pulpy, about 5 minutes. Transfer to a serving bowl.

Serve the *chili rajas* as a garnish or topping for pilafs, tostadas, burritos, tortas, or quesadillas.

Makes six ½-cup servings

Per serving:
33 Calories; 1g Protein; 2g Fat;
5g Carbohydrates; 0 Cholesterol;
197mg Sodium; 1g Fiber

Pepitas

TOASTED PUMPKIN SEEDS

Toasted pumpkin seeds are a healthy Mexican snack.

**1 cup raw pumpkin seeds
(see Helpful Hint)**
½ teaspoon salt
¼ teaspoon cayenne pepper

Add the seeds to a hot, ungreased skillet. Cook, stirring, over medium heat until the seeds are lightly toasted and popping like popcorn, about 3 minutes. Remove from the heat and sprinkle in the salt and cayenne pepper. Transfer to a serving bowl and serve as a light snack.

Makes four ¼-cup servings

Helpful Hint

Generally speaking, there are two kinds of pumpkin seeds sold in U.S. supermarkets. The unsalted raw pumpkin seeds are dark green and ideally used for cooking and home-made snacks. Most white seeds have already been commercially roasted and salted and are intended for snacking.

Per serving:
186 Calories; 8g Protein; 10g Fat;
6g Carbohydrates; 0 Cholesterol;
152mg Sodium; 5g Fiber

Orange-Avocado Relish

A squeeze of fresh orange gives this avocado condiment a citrusy twist.

1 ripe avocado, peeled, pitted, and diced (see Helpful Hints, page 11)
1 tomato, finely chopped
¼ cup finely chopped red onion
¼ cup jarred roasted red peppers, diced
2 whole scallions, trimmed and chopped
2 tablespoons chopped cilantro (optional)
Juice of 1 orange
½ teaspoon salt
½ teaspoon freshly ground black pepper

Place all of the ingredients in a mixing bowl and toss together. Transfer to a serving bowl and serve as an accompaniment to burritos, quesadillas, or as a topping for tostadas.

Makes 2 cups
(Eight ¼-cup servings)

Per serving:
54 Calories; 1g Protein; 3g Fat; 6g Carbohydrates; 0 Cholesterol; 149mg Sodium; 3g Fiber

Smoky Guacamole

Ripe avocados make the tastiest, richest guacamoles—be sure to use them. Chipotle chilies give this dip a smoky nuance.

2 ripe avocados, peeled, pitted, and diced (see Helpful Hints, page 11)
1 ripe tomato, diced
¼ cup finely chopped red onion
2 cloves garlic, minced
2 whole scallions, trimmed and chopped
1 canned chipotle chili, minced
2 tablespoons chopped cilantro
Juice of 1 lime
½ teaspoon ground cumin
½ teaspoon salt
½ teaspoon freshly ground black pepper

Place all of the ingredients in a medium mixing bowl and mash together with a spoon or potato masher. Transfer the dip to a serving bowl and serve at once with tortilla chips or raw vegetables. You can also serve guacamole as a condiment for burritos or tostadas.

Makes 2 cups
(Eight ¼-cup servings)

Per serving:
86 Calories; 1g Protein; 8g Fat;
5g Carbohydrates; 0 Cholesterol;
158mg Sodium; 2g Fiber

Ultimate Black Bean Dip

*This scrumptious bean dip is a healthful alternative
to sour cream or cream cheese concoctions.*

One 15-ounce can black beans
1 tablespoon canola oil
1 small yellow onion, diced
1 tomato, diced
2 cloves garlic, minced
1 tablespoon chopped pickled
    jalapeños (optional)
2 whole scallions, trimmed
    and chopped
1½ teaspoons dried oregano
1 teaspoon ground cumin
½ teaspoon freshly ground
    black pepper

Drain the beans, reserving ¼ cup of the liquid.

In a medium saucepan, heat the oil over medium heat. Add the onion, tomato, garlic, and jalapeños if desired and cook, stirring, until tender, about 5 minutes. Add the black beans and reserved liquid, and the remaining ingredients, and cook 7 to 9 minutes, stirring occasionally.

Transfer the bean mixture to a blender or food processor fitted with a steel blade and process until smooth, about 5 seconds. Pour the pureed mixture into a serving bowl. Serve with warm flour tortillas, pita, or with raw vegetables. The dip can also be used as a topping for tostadas or quesadillas.

Makes about 2 cups
(Eight ¼-cup servings)

Per serving:
52 Calories; 2g Protein; 2g Fat;
9g Carbohydrates; 0 Cholesterol;
210mg Sodium; 3g Fiber

Poblano-Cilantro Hummus

Poblano chilies give this chickpea dip a delectable roasted flavor.

2 fresh poblano chilies, cored and seeded
One 15-ounce can chickpeas
¼ cup tahini (sesame seed paste)
Juice of 1 lemon
2 large cloves garlic, minced
2 tablespoons chopped fresh parsley
2 tablespoons chopped cilantro
1 teaspoon ground cumin
½ teaspoon salt
¼ teaspoon cayenne pepper

Roast the chilies by placing them over an open flame or beneath a broiler until the skin is charred, 4 to 6 minutes on each side. Remove the chilies from the heat and let cool for a few minutes.

With a butter knife (or your hands—wear rubber gloves to protect your skin), scrape the charred skin from the flesh and discard. Remove the seeds and chop the flesh.

Meanwhile, drain the chickpeas, reserving about ¼ cup of the liquid. Add the chilies, chickpeas, and reserved liquid along with the remaining ingredients to a blender or food processor fitted with a steel blade and process until smooth, about 10 seconds. Stop to scrape the sides with a spatula at least once or twice.

Transfer the hummus to a serving bowl and serve with flour tortillas and/or raw vegetables.

Makes 2 cups
(Eight ¼-cup servings)

Per serving:
116 Calories; 4g Protein; 4g Fat; 12g Carbohydrates; 0 Cholesterol; 420mg Sodium; 4g Fiber

Party-Time Nachos

Thanks to baked tortilla chips, low-fat yogurt, and vegetarian refried beans, these nachos prove that "healthy party food" is not a contradiction in terms.

One 16-ounce can vegetarian refried beans
4 ounces baked tortilla chips (about ½ bag)
½ cup tomato salsa
⅓ cup low-fat plain yogurt
2 large whole scallions, trimmed and chopped
2 tablespoons pickled jalapeño slices (optional)

Place the refried beans in a medium saucepan. Cook over medium-high heat, stirring, until steaming, 4 to 5 minutes. Set aside.

Arrange the tortilla chips in the center of a round serving plate, forming a mound. Ladle the refried beans over the center of the chips. Spoon the salsa and yogurt over the top of the beans. Sprinkle the scallions and jalapeño slices if desired over the top. Place the nachos in the center of the table and serve as a casual appetizer.

Makes 4 servings

Per serving:
228 Calories; 9g Protein; 5g Fat; 36g Carbohydrates; 9mg Cholesterol; 910mg Sodium; 7g Fiber

Wild Mushroom Tostadas with Feta

*Wild mushrooms and TVP (textured vegetable protein)
replace the meat in this inventive appetizer.*

2 tablespoons dry wine
  (red or white)
1 tablespoon canola oil
8 ounces fresh shiitake or
  oyster mushrooms,
  chopped
4 ounces fresh white mushrooms, chopped
1 medium yellow onion, finely
  chopped
2 large cloves garlic, minced
1 cup TVP (textured vegetable
  protein), mince-style
1 cup vegetable stock or water
2 tablespoons commercial
  taco seasoning (see
  Helpful Hint)
6 tostada shells
About ½ cup tomato salsa or
  taco sauce
6 to 8 romaine leaves, cut into
  ribbons (chiffonade-style)
4 whole scallions, trimmed and
  chopped
2 ounces feta cheese, crumbled
  (optional)

Preheat the oven to 350°F.

In a medium saucepan, heat the wine and oil over medium heat. Add the mushrooms, onion, and garlic and cook, stirring, until tender, 6 to 7 minutes. Add the TVP, vegetable stock, and taco seasoning and bring to a simmer. Reduce heat to medium-low and cook, stirring frequently, about 10 minutes.

Arrange the tostada shells on two baking pans. Bake until crisp, 4 to 6 minutes. Remove from the oven and arrange on a large serving platter. Spread 2 to 3 tablespoons of the mushroom mixture over each tostada. Top with the salsa, romaine, scallions, and feta cheese if desired. Serve the tostadas immediately.

**Makes 6 tostadas
(6 servings)**

Helpful Hint

If commercial taco seasoning is unavailable, substitute 1 teaspoon chili powder and ½ teaspoon each of salt, black pepper, garlic powder, and cumin.

Per serving:
281 Calories; 16g Protein; 10g Fat;
35g Carbohydrates; 0 Cholesterol;
813mg Sodium; 5g Fiber

Guacamole Tostadas

*The medley of guacamole, refried beans, and romaine
lettuce makes for a delightful topping.*

**One 15-ounce can black beans
  or pinto beans**
2 teaspoons canola oil
1 small yellow onion, diced
**1 tablespoon commercial taco
  seasoning (see Helpful Hint,
  page 19)**
**2 ripe avocados, peeled, pitted,
  and diced (see Helpful
  Hints, page 11)**
2 plum tomatoes, chopped
**2 whole scallions, trimmed and
  chopped**
2 tablespoons chopped cilantro
1 large clove garlic, minced
Juice of 1 lime
½ teaspoon ground cumin
8 tostada shells
**6 to 8 romaine leaves, cut into
  ribbons (chiffonade-style)**

Preheat the oven to 350°F.

Drain the beans, reserving
¼ cup of the liquid. In a medium
saucepan, heat the oil over medium heat. Add the onion and
cook, stirring, until tender,
about 4 minutes. Reduce the
heat to medium-low and add
the beans, reserved liquid, and
taco seasoning. Cook, stirring,
about 6 minutes. Transfer the
bean mixture to a blender or a
food processor fitted with a steel
blade and process until smooth,
about 5 seconds, stopping to
stir at least once. Return the
pureed beans to the pan and cook,
stirring, over low heat for another
5 minutes.

Place the avocados, tomatoes,
scallions, cilantro, garlic, lime
juice, and cumin in a medium
mixing bowl and toss together.
Set aside.

Arrange the tostada shells on
two baking pans. Bake until crisp,
4 to 6 minutes. Remove from the
oven and arrange on a large
serving platter. Spread 3 to 4
tablespoons of the bean mixture
on each tostada. Top with the
romaine and then the guacamole.
Serve the tostadas at once.

**Makes 8 tostadas
(8 servings)**

Per serving:
276 Calories; 6g Protein; 15g Fat;
33g Carbohydrates; 0 Cholesterol;
288mg Sodium; 7g Fiber

Artichoke Tostada Mini-Pizzas

*This appetizer springs from the happy marriage of
Italian pizza and Mexican tostadas.*

1 cup chunky tomato salsa
**2 tablespoons chopped fresh
   basil**
**28 ounces refrigerated pizza
   dough, thawed to room
   temperature**
**One 14-ounce can artichoke
   hearts, drained and
   coarsely chopped**
**1 cup cooked red kidney
   beans or black beans,
   well drained**
**¾ cup shredded low-fat
   Monterey Jack or
   mozzarella cheese**

Preheat the oven to 375°F.

In a small mixing bowl, combine the salsa and basil. Set aside.

Divide the dough into 6 equal-size balls. On a flat work surface, roll out the balls of dough into circles and place onto two lightly greased baking pans. Spread the salsa mixture evenly over the top of each circle, leaving a half-inch of dough at the edge. Spread the artichokes and beans evenly over the salsa and top each pizza with about 2 tablespoons of shredded cheese.

Bake until the crusts are light brown and the cheese is bubbling, 15 to 20 minutes. Remove from the oven and cool for about 5 minutes before serving.

Makes 6 servings

Helpful Hint

*For best results, make the tostada
pizzas with a chunky commercial or
homemade salsa.*

Per serving:
457 Calories; 20g Protein; 8g Fat;
76g Carbohydrates; 10mg Cholesterol; 1,207mg Sodium; 9g Fiber

Hummus Tostadas with Jalapeño Peppers

*Hummus, the eminent Middle Eastern spread, makes a
natural cross-cultural topping for Mexican tostadas.*

One 15-ounce can chickpeas
**¼ cup tahini (sesame seed
    paste)**
Juice of 1 lemon
2 cloves garlic, minced
¼ cup chopped fresh parsley
½ teaspoon ground cumin
½ teaspoon salt
**½ teaspoon freshly ground
    black pepper**
8 tostada shells
**6 to 8 romaine leaves, cut into
    ribbons (chiffonade-style)**
2 tomatoes, diced
¼ cup pickled jalapeño slices

Preheat the oven to 350°F.

Drain the chickpeas and
reserve ¼ cup of the liquid.
Add the chickpeas, chickpea
liquid, tahini, lemon juice, garlic,
parsley, cumin, salt, and pepper
to a blender or food processor
fitted with a steel blade and
process until smooth, about 10
seconds. Transfer to a small bowl.

Arrange the tostada shells on
two baking pans. Bake until crisp,
4 to 6 minutes. Remove shells from
the oven and arrange on a large
serving platter. Spread 2 to 3
tablespoons of hummus over
each tostada. Top the hummus
with the romaine, tomatoes, and
jalapeño slices. Serve the tostadas
immediately.

**Makes 8 tostadas
(8 servings)**

Per serving:
262 Calories, 7g Protein; 13g Fat;
31g Carbohydrates; 0 Cholesterol;
347mg Sodium; 3g Fiber

Mesclun and Black Bean Tostadas

*Mesclun, a mix of salad greens, adds a touch (and taste)
of panache to this humble Mexican appetizer.*

**One 15-ounce can black beans,
undrained**
2 teaspoons canola oil
1 small yellow onion, diced
**1 tablespoon commercial taco
seasoning (see Helpful Hint,
page 19)**
6 tostada shells
**6 tablespoons shredded low-fat
Monterey Jack or Swiss
cheese**
3 to 4 ounces mesclun
2 plum tomatoes, diced
1 small red onion, chopped

Preheat the oven to 350°F.

Drain the beans, reserving
¼ cup of the liquid.

In a medium saucepan, heat
the oil over medium heat. Add
the onion and cook, stirring,
until tender, about 4 minutes.
Add the beans, bean liquid,
and taco seasoning; reduce heat
to medium-low and cook, stirring, until beans are heated
through, about 6 minutes.
Transfer three-quarters of the
beans to a blender or food processor fitted with a steel blade
and process until smooth, about
5 seconds, stopping to stir at least
once. Return the beans to the pan;
reduce heat to low, and cook,
stirring, until heated through,
about 5 minutes.

Meanwhile, arrange the tostada
shells on a large baking pan. Bake
until crisp, 4 to 6 minutes. Remove from the oven and arrange
on a large serving platter.

Spread about ¼ cup of the bean
mixture on each tostada. Top each
with 1 tablespoon cheese and
evenly distribute the mesclun,
tomatoes, and red onion over the
bean mixture. Serve the tostadas
immediately.

**Makes 6 tostadas
(6 servings)**

Per serving:
231 Calories; 7g Protein; 10g Fat;
30g Carbohydrates; 5mg Cholesterol; 403mg Sodium; 4g Fiber

Sweet Potato Tostadas

These irresistible tostadas are topped with mashed sweet potatoes. A hint of molasses brings out the natural sweetness of the potatoes.

About 2 medium sweet potatoes, peeled and diced (3 cups)
½ cup warmed skim milk or soy milk
1 tablespoon molasses
1 teaspoon paprika
½ teaspoon salt
¼ teaspoon cayenne pepper
6 tostada shells
6 to 8 romaine leaves, cut into ribbons (chiffonade-style)
½ cup tomato salsa or taco sauce
½ cup low-fat plain yogurt

Preheat the oven to 350°F.

In a medium saucepan, bring about 2 quarts of water to a boil. Place the sweet potatoes in the boiling water and cook over medium heat until tender, stirring occasionally, about 15 minutes. Drain in a colander and transfer to a mixing bowl.

Add the milk, molasses, paprika, salt, and cayenne to the sweet potatoes. Mash with a large fork or potato masher until ingredients are blended. Keep warm until the tostada shells are ready.

Meanwhile, arrange the tostada shells on two baking pans. Bake 4 to 6 minutes. Remove from the oven and arrange on a large serving platter. Spread ¼ cup of the mashed sweet potatoes over each tostada. Top with the romaine, salsa, and yogurt and serve.

**Makes 6 tostadas
(6 servings)**

Per serving:
28 Calories; 4g Protein; 8g Fat; 30g Carbohydrates; 1mg Cholesterol; 376mg Sodium; 1g Fiber

Potato Cheese Empanaditas

Serve these "baby" empanadas as a finger food or light snack. They take a little longer than 30 minutes to prepare, but they're worth it.

3 cups peeled and coarsely chopped white potatoes
⅓ cup low-fat milk or soy milk
½ teaspoon salt
¼ teaspoon white pepper
½ cup shredded Monterey Jack cheese
12 ounces commercial bread dough (preferably dinner roll dough)

In a medium saucepan, bring about 2 quarts of water to a boil. Add the potatoes and cook over medium heat until tender, about 20 minutes, stirring occasionally. Drain in a colander.

Transfer the potatoes to a medium mixing bowl. Stir in the milk, salt, and white pepper. With a potato masher or fork, mash the potatoes together. (It's okay to leave few small lumps.) Blend in the cheese.

Preheat the oven to 375°F. Form the bread dough into 8 small balls. (If using precut or "scored" dinner rolls, simply pull the rolls apart.) With your fingers, flatten each ball into a circle. Spoon about 2 tablespoons of the mashed potatoes into the center of each circle. Fold over the edges, forming a crescent-shaped turnover or small empanada.

Arrange the empanaditas on a large baking pan. Bake until the rolls are lightly browned, 13 to 15 minutes. Remove from the heat and transfer to a serving platter. Serve with condiments such as salsa, guacamole, or taco sauce.

Makes 8 empanaditas
(8 servings)

Per serving:
163 Calories; 5g Protein; 5g Fat; 24g Carbohydrates; 11mg Cholesterol; 436mg Sodium; 1g Fiber

Molletes

OPEN FACE CHEESE MELTS

*These Mexican "street snacks" are delightfully delicious
and incredibly easy to make.*

**One 16-ounce can refried black
  beans**
4 crusty French rolls
1 cup tomato salsa
**1 to 2 tablespoons pickled
  jalapeños (optional)**
**½ cup shredded Monterey Jack
  cheese**

Add the refried beans to a medium saucepan. Cook, stirring, over medium heat until steaming, 4 to 5 minutes. Set aside.

Preheat the broiler.

Slice the rolls in half. Arrange the rolls on a baking pan, cut-side facing up. Spoon 1 to 2 tablespoons of refried beans over the top of each side. Top with the salsa, jalapeños if desired, and cheese. Broil until the cheese melts, about 2 minutes. Remove from the oven and transfer to a serving platter. Serve at once.

Makes 4 servings

VARIATIONS

*Toppings can include guacamole,
chopped scallions, chili rajas,
or salsa verde.*

Per serving:
374 Calories; 16g Protein; 9g Fat;
61g Carbohydrates; 15mg Cholesterol; 1,234mg Sodium; 10g Fiber

CHAPTER 2

Soups and Salads

Summery Garden Gazpacho

Here's a cold and nourishing soup for a hot, balmy day.

2 cups canned tomato juice
2 tomatoes, diced
1 small red onion, chopped
1 sweet Italian pepper, seeded
  and diced
1 cucumber, peeled and diced
2 cloves garlic, minced
2 tablespoons chopped fresh
  parsley
½ teaspoon ground cumin
½ teaspoon salt
½ teaspoon freshly ground
  black pepper
¼ teaspoon red pepper flakes

In a large mixing bowl, combine all of the ingredients. Place three-quarters of the mixture in a blender or food processor fitted with a steel blade and process, forming a vegetable mash, about 5 seconds. Return to the bowl and blend with the remaining vegetable mixture. Chill for 15 to 30 minutes before serving.

To serve, ladle the gazpacho into chilled bowls and serve with warm flour tortillas.

Makes 4 servings

VARIATIONS

For an appealing presentation, garnish the gazpacho with chopped scallions, shredded carrots, and/or a dollop of low-fat plain yogurt.

Per serving:
61 Calories; 3g Protein; 0 Fat;
14g Carbohydrates; 0 Cholesterol;
726mg Sodium; 3g Fiber

Avocado and Black Bean Gazpacho

2 cups canned tomato juice
2 tomatoes, diced
1 small red onion, chopped
1 red bell pepper, seeded
    and diced
1 cucumber, peeled and diced
2 cloves garlic, minced
2 tablespoons chopped cilantro
½ teaspoon ground cumin
½ teaspoon salt
½ teaspoon freshly ground
    black pepper
¼ teaspoon red pepper flakes
Juice of 1 lime
1 ripe avocado, peeled, pitted,
    and diced (see Helpful
    Hints, page 11)
1 cup cooked or canned black
    beans, drained well

In a large mixing bowl, combine all of the ingredients except the avocado and black beans. Place three-quarters of the mixture in a blender or food processor fitted with a steel blade and process, forming a vegetable mash, about 5 seconds. Return to the bowl and blend with the remaining vegetable mixture. Mix in the avocado and black beans and chill for 15 to 30 minutes before serving.

Ladle the gazpacho into chilled bowls and serve with warm flour tortillas.

Makes 4 to 6 servings

VARIATIONS

Garnish the gazpacho with chopped scallions, roasted corn kernels, or low-fat plain yogurt.

Per serving:
189 Calories; 7g Protein; 8g Fat;
26g Carbohydrates; 0 Cholesterol;
731mg Sodium; 8g Fiber

Sopa de Tortilla

TORTILLA SOUP

Like the bread soups of Italian fame, strips of tortillas often find their way into Mexican sopas. It's also a tasty way to use up any leftover tortillas.

1 tablespoon canola oil
1 medium yellow onion, diced
1 small zucchini, diced
1 green bell pepper, seeded and diced
2 large cloves garlic, minced
1 tablespoon chopped pickled jalapeños, (optional)
6 cups water or vegetable broth
½ cup tomato paste
1 large white potato, peeled and diced
1 tablespoon dried oregano
1½ teaspoons ground cumin
½ teaspoon salt
One 15-ounce can red kidney beans, drained
One 15-ounce can corn kernels, drained
Four 6-inch corn or flour tortillas, cut into ½-inch-wide strips

In a large saucepan, heat the oil over medium heat. Add the onion, zucchini, bell pepper, garlic, and jalapeños if desired and cook, stirring, until tender, about 7 minutes. Add the water, tomato paste, potato, oregano, cumin, and salt and bring to a simmer. Cook until the potato is tender, about 15 minutes, stirring occasionally. Stir in the beans, corn, and tortilla strips and cook, stirring occasionally, for 5 minutes.

Ladle into bowls and serve at once.

Makes 6 servings

VARIATIONS

For a refreshing garnish, top the soup with a few tablespoons of chopped cilantro, parsley, or scallions.

Per serving:
198 Calories; 8g Protein; 3g Fat; 37g Carbohydrates; 0 Cholesterol; 592mg Sodium; 7g Fiber

Sizzling Black Bean Soup

1 tablespoon canola oil

1 medium yellow onion, diced

1 green bell pepper, seeded
and diced

2 ribs celery, chopped

Two 15-ounce cans black beans,
drained

1 cup canned crushed tomatoes

1 cup water or vegetable broth

2 tablespoons chopped fresh
parsley

1 tablespoon chopped pickled
jalapeños

1 tablespoon chili powder

2 teaspoons dried oregano

1½ teaspoons ground cumin

½ teaspoon salt

In a large saucepan, heat the oil over medium heat. Add the onion, bell pepper, and celery and cook, stirring, until tender, about 5 minutes. Add the remaining ingredients and bring to a simmer. Cook for 15 minutes over medium-low heat, stirring occasionally. Transfer to a blender or food processor fitted with a steel blade and puree until smooth, about 5 seconds.

Ladle the soup into bowls and serve at once.

Makes 4 servings

VARIATIONS

Add 2 or 3 tablespoons of chopped cilantro to the soup a few minutes before serving. Low-fat plain yogurt makes a soothing topping.

Per serving:
175 Calories; 9g Protein; 4g Fat;
34g Carbohydrates; 0 Cholesterol;
1,239mg Sodium; 11g Fiber

Sopa de Fideo
MEXICAN NOODLE SOUP

Fideo, which means "noodle," adds sustenance to this soup, a distant cousin of Italian pasta fagioli.

1 tablespoon canola oil
1 medium yellow onion, diced
1 red bell pepper, seeded
   and diced
2 ribs celery, chopped
2 medium carrots, peeled
   and diced
3 to 4 cloves garlic, minced
6 cups water or vegetable
   broth
1 large white potato, peeled
   and diced
1 tablespoon dried parsley
1 tablespoon dried oregano
1½ teaspoons ground cumin
1 teaspoon salt
½ teaspoon freshly ground
   black pepper
4 ounces spaghetti or linguine,
   snapped in half
½ cup tomato paste

In a large saucepan, heat the oil over medium heat. Add the onion, bell pepper, celery, carrots, and garlic and cook, stirring, until tender, about 7 minutes. Add the water, potato, parsley, oregano, cumin, salt, and pepper and bring to a simmer. Cook for 12 minutes over medium heat, stirring occasionally.

Stir the pasta and tomato paste into the soup. Cook until the pasta is *al dente,* about 10 minutes, stirring occasionally. Let the soup stand for a few minutes before serving.

Ladle the soup into bowls. If desired, serve with warm tortillas on the side.

Makes 6 servings

Per serving:
151 Calories; 5g Protein; 3g Fat;
28g Carbohydrates; 0 Cholesterol;
424mg Sodium; 3g Fiber

Zucchini-Nopales Soup

*Nopales, or cactus paddles, are oval, paddlelike leaves of the cactus plant.
A favored ingredient in soups and stews, nopales have an okralike texture
and a taste reminiscent of green beans.*

**2 medium nopales (see Helpful
Hint)**
2 teaspoons canola oil
1 medium yellow onion, diced
1 zucchini, diced
2 to 3 cloves garlic, minced
4 cups vegetable broth
**One 14-ounce can stewed
tomatoes, undrained**
**1 white potato, peeled and
diced**
2 teaspoons dried oregano
1 teaspoon dried basil
½ teaspoon salt
**½ teaspoon freshly ground
black pepper**
½ cup tomato paste

To prepare the nopales, scrape off
the prickly needles and bumps.
(Careful: The needles are sharp.)
Cut off the base and trim around
the outer edge of the paddle. Cut
the paddles in half across the
width, then cut into ¼-inch-wide
strips. The strips should resemble
green beans.

In a medium saucepan, heat
the oil over medium heat. Add the
onion, zucchini, and garlic, and
cook, stirring, until the onion is
translucent, about 5 minutes. Add
the vegetable broth, tomatoes and
liquid, potato, oregano, basil, salt,
and pepper and bring to a simmer.
Cook over medium heat, stirring
occasionally, about 10 minutes.
Stir in the nopales and tomato
paste and cook until the nopales
and potatoes are tender, stirring
occasionally, 10 to 15 minutes.
Let stand for 5 minutes before
serving.

Ladle the soup into bowls and
serve with warm flour tortillas.

Makes 6 servings

Helpful Hint

*Do not be intimidated by the prickly
needles on nopales; they are easily
scraped off with a sharp knife.*

Per serving:
139 Calories; 5g Protein; 3g Fat;
28g Carbohydrates; 0 Cholesterol;
1,136 mg Sodium; 5g Fiber

Cumin-Scented Sweet Potato Bisque

The earthy fragrance of cumin and a slight twang from jalapeños and cilantro imbue this sweet potato soup with a Mexican personality.

1 tablespoon canola oil
1 medium yellow onion, diced
1 red bell pepper, seeded and diced
1 large rib celery, chopped
2 large cloves garlic, minced
1 jalapeño pepper, seeded and minced
4 cups water or vegetable broth
4 cups peeled and coarsely chopped sweet potatoes
2 teaspoons paprika
1½ teaspoons ground cumin
½ teaspoon salt
½ teaspoon white pepper
1 cup whole or low-fat milk or soy milk
2 tablespoons chopped cilantro

In a large saucepan, heat the oil over medium heat. Add the onion, bell pepper, celery, garlic, and jalapeño and cook, stirring, until the onions are translucent, about 6 minutes. Add the water, potatoes, paprika, cumin, salt, and white pepper and bring to a simmer. Cook, stirring occasionally, over medium-low heat until the potatoes are tender, about 20 minutes.

Transfer the soup to a blender or food processor fitted with a steel blade and process until smooth, about 5 seconds. Return the soup to the pan and stir in the milk and cilantro. Bring the soup to a gentle simmer.

Ladle the bisque into bowls and serve at once.

Makes 6 servings

Per serving:
94 Calories; 2g Protein; 4g Fat; 12g Carbohydrates; 5mg Cholesterol; 286mg Sodium; 2g Fiber

Cascabel Potato Soup

This soothing potato soup is enhanced with dried cascabel chilies, dark mahogany pods with a bulbous shape. Cascabel means "rattle"; the seeds make a rattlelike sound when shaken.

4 to 6 dried cascabel chilies
2 teaspoons canola oil
1 medium yellow onion, diced
2 red bell peppers, seeded
  and diced
3 to 4 cloves garlic, minced
4 cups water or vegetable
  broth
2½ cups peeled and diced
  white potatoes
1 large carrot, peeled and diced
½ teaspoon salt
½ teaspoon white pepper
1 cup whole or low-fat milk
2 tablespoons chopped cilantro

In a large bowl, cover the chilies with simmering hot water and soak until soft, 15 to 20 minutes. Place a lid or plate over the chilies to keep them from floating. Drain the chilies, remove the seeds, and chop the flesh. Set aside.

In a large saucepan, heat the oil over medium-high heat. Add the onion, bell peppers, and garlic and cook, stirring, until the onion is translucent, about 5 minutes. Add the water, potatoes, carrot, salt, white pepper, and chilies and bring to a simmer. Cook over medium-low heat until the potatoes are tender, about 20 minutes, stirring occasionally.

Transfer the soup to a blender or food processor fitted with a steel blade and process until smooth, about 5 seconds. Return to the pan and stir in the milk and cilantro. Bring to a gentle simmer. Ladle the soup into bowls and serve at once.

Makes 6 servings

Per serving:
114 Calories; 3g Protein; 3g Fat; 19g Carbohydrates; 5mg Cholesterol; 226mg Sodium; 3g Fiber

Asparagus, Corn, and Rice Salad

Mexico's two most popular grains, rice and corn, team up with asparagus in this lime-scented salad.

2 tablespoons red wine vinegar
2 tablespoons canola oil
Juice of 1 lime
1 tablespoon chopped pickled
  jalapeños
¼ cup chopped fresh parsley
2 tablespoons chopped cilantro
  (optional)
½ teaspoon salt
½ teaspoon freshly ground
  black pepper
3 cups cooked long-grain white
  rice or brown rice (see
  Helpful Hint)
12 asparagus spears, blanched
  and cut into 1-inch pieces
One 15-ounce can corn kernels,
  drained
2 plum tomatoes, diced
3 to 4 whole scallions, chopped

In a large mixing bowl, whisk together the vinegar, oil, lime juice, jalapeños, parsley, cilantro if desired, salt, and pepper. Stir in the remaining ingredients. Chill the salad for 30 minutes to 1 hour before serving.

For an appealing presentation, serve the salad over a bed of dark leafy greens.

Makes 4 servings

Helpful Hint

For 3 cups of cooked rice, combine about 1¼ cups uncooked rice with 2½ cups water and cook, covered, until tender.

Per serving:
328 Calories; 8g Protein; 9g Fat;
58g Carbohydrates; 0 Cholesterol;
670mg Sodium; 4g Fiber

Calabacitas and Jicama Salad with Chipotle-Lime Dressing

The term calabacitas *loosely refers to a variety of summer squash; sometimes it also describes a medley of vegetables.* Calabacita *is not to be confused with* calabaza, *the name for a hard-shelled pumpkin popular in Caribbean cooking. When summer squash are small to medium in size, they are tender enough to serve raw in marinated salads.*

1 small zucchini, diced
1 small yellow summer squash, diced
2 carrots, peeled and shredded
1 cup peeled and diced jicama
One 11-ounce can corn kernels, drained
Juice of 2 limes
2 tablespoons canola oil
1 canned chipotle chile, seeded and minced
2 tablespoons minced cilantro
½ teaspoon ground cumin
½ teaspoon salt

Combine all of the ingredients in a medium mixing bowl and blend together thoroughly. Refrigerate for 15 to 30 minutes to allow the flavors to meld together.

Serve the salad over a bed of leaf lettuce.

Makes 4 servings

Per serving:
162 Calories; 4g Protein; 7g Fat; 25g Carbohydrates; 0 Cholesterol; 316mg Sodium; 6g Fiber

Mexicali Pasta Salad

This festive pasta salad includes the staples of the Mexican kitchen. For an interesting twist, try a specialty pasta made with corn flour.

8 ounces corn spirals or Italian pasta spirals

2 tablespoons canola oil

2 tablespoons apple cider vinegar

2 large cloves garlic, minced

Juice of 2 limes

¼ cup chopped fresh parsley

2 teaspoons dried oregano

½ teaspoon salt

½ teaspoon freshly ground black pepper

12 to 14 cherry tomatoes, halved

4 whole scallions, trimmed and chopped

One 15-ounce can red chili beans, drained

One 11-ounce can corn kernels, drained

In a large saucepan, bring 2½ quarts of water to a boil over medium-high heat. Add the pasta spirals to the boiling water, stir, and return to a boil. Cook until *al dente,* stirring occasionally, about 5 minutes. (If using semolina pasta, cook about 10 minutes.) Drain the pasta in a colander and cool under cold running water.

Meanwhile, in a large mixing bowl, whisk together the oil, vinegar, garlic, lime juice, parsley, oregano, salt, and pepper. Add the cooked pasta and the remaining ingredients and toss together. Serve now or refrigerate for later. (Ideally, the salad should be refrigerated for 15 to 30 minutes to allow the flavors to meld.)

Makes 6 servings

Per serving:
258 Calories, 8g Protein; 6g Fat; 48g Carbohydrates; 0 Cholesterol; 581mg Sodium; 9g Fiber

Artichoke, Rice, and Lime Salad

Fresh limes, staples of the Mexican pantry, offer a tangy, low-fat flavor to this light salad of artichokes, rice, and vegetables.

2½ cups cooked long-grain white rice or brown rice (see Helpful Hint)
One 15-ounce can artichoke hearts, drained and coarsely chopped
One 14-ounce can corn kernels, drained
4 whole scallions, trimmed and chopped
½ cup jarred roasted red peppers, cut in narrow strips
1 small cucumber, peeled and diced
1 jalapeño or chipotle chili, seeded and minced (optional)
2 tablespoons canola oil
Juice of 2 limes
2 to 3 tablespoons chopped cilantro
2 teaspoons dried oregano
1 teaspoon ground cumin
½ teaspoon salt
½ teaspoon freshly ground black pepper

In a large mixing bowl, combine all of the ingredients and mix thoroughly. Chill for at least 15 to 30 minutes to allow the flavors to meld.

Fluff the salad with a fork before serving. To serve, spoon the salad over a bed of green lettuce. If desired, offer a rolled flour tortilla on the side.

Makes 6 servings

Helpful Hint

For 2½ cups of cooked rice, combine about 1 cup uncooked rice with 2 cups water and cook, covered, until tender.

Per serving:
196 Calories; 5g Protein; 5g Fat; 33g Carbohydrates; 0 Cholesterol; 495mg Sodium; 2g Fiber

Mexican Tabbouleh

An inspired Mexican twist on the Middle Eastern wheat garden salad.

1 cup fine bulgur
2 cups boiling water
2 tomatoes, diced
1 cucumber, peeled and diced
One 15-ounce can black beans
or pinto beans, drained
One 11-ounce can corn kernels,
drained
2 whole scallions, trimmed and
chopped
½ cup chopped fresh parsley
2 tablespoons chopped cilantro
Juice of 1½ to 2 lemons
2 tablespoons olive oil
½ teaspoon salt
½ teaspoon freshly ground
black pepper
1 to 2 serrano chilies, seeded
and minced (optional)

Combine the bulgur and boiling water in a saucepan or bowl and cover. Let sit until most of the water is absorbed, about 15 minutes. Drain the excess liquid.

Meanwhile, in a medium mixing bowl, combine the remaining ingredients. When the bulgur is ready, toss with the bean mixture. Serve now as a warm salad or chill for later.

To serve, spoon the tabbouleh over a bed of leafy greens. If desired, offer warm flour tortillas on the side.

Makes 6 servings

Per serving:
218 Calories; 8g Protein; 5g Fat;
42g Carbohydrates; 0 Cholesterol;
498mg Sodium; 10g Fiber

Jicama Cabbage Salad

Crisp jicama blends with cabbage and carrots for a coleslaw-style salad.

**2 cups peeled and shredded
  jicama**
2 cups shredded red cabbage
2 carrots, peeled and shredded
**½ cup low-fat ranch dressing or
  coleslaw dressing**
**1 tablespoon minced pickled
  jalapeño peppers (optional)**
½ teaspoon celery seeds

Combine all of the ingredients in a medium mixing bowl and blend thoroughly. Chill for 10 to 15 minutes before serving.

Serve as a light side dish or side salad.

Makes 4 servings

Per serving:
114 Calories; 1g Protein; 6g Fat;
14g Carbohydrates; 0 Cholesterol;
280mg Sodium; 5g Fiber

Lime Couscous Salad
with Black Beans and Corn

The trio of Mexican flavors—cilantro, jalapeños, and lime—brings an aromatic taste to this fulfilling salad of couscous, beans, and corn.

1 cup couscous
1½ cups boiling water
1 tomato, diced
4 whole scallions, trimmed
    and chopped
One 15-ounce can black beans,
    drained
One 14-ounce can corn kernels,
    drained
2 tablespoons chopped cilantro
1 tablespoon chopped pickled
    jalapeños
1 tablespoon canola oil
1 teaspoon dried oregano
½ teaspoon salt
½ teaspoon freshly ground
    black pepper
Juice of 2 limes

In a medium bowl or saucepan, combine the couscous and boiling water. Cover and let stand for 10 minutes. Fluff the grains with a fork.

In a mixing bowl, combine the couscous with the remaining ingredients and toss together thoroughly. Chill for 15 minutes before serving to allow the flavors to meld. Serve as a side salad or as a filling for a burrito or pita.

Makes 4 servings

Per serving:
335 Calories; 12g Protein; 5g Fat;
67g Carbohydrates; 0 Cholesterol;
954mg Sodium; 9g Fiber

Avocado, Corn, and Bean Salad

This artsy, picturesque salad can be ready in minutes and is a snap to make. Avocados bring a luscious flavor to the humble combination of beans and corn.

One 15-ounce can black beans, drained
One 15-ounce can corn kernels, drained
4 whole scallions, trimmed and chopped
2 tomatoes, diced
1 ripe avocado, peeled, pitted, and diced (see Helpful Hints, page 11)
½ cup jarred roasted red peppers, diced
2 tablespoons canola oil
Juice of 2 limes
¼ cup chopped fresh parsley
2 teaspoons dried oregano
½ teaspoon salt
½ teaspoon freshly ground black pepper

Combine all of the ingredients in a large mixing bowl and blend well, being careful not to mash the avocado. Refrigerate the salad for 15 to 30 minutes to allow the flavors to meld. Serve as a cold side dish or as a light salad.

Makes 6 servings

VARIATION

If desired, add 3 to 4 tablespoons chopped cilantro to the salad.

Per serving:
175 Calories; 5g Protein; 10g Fat; 22g Carbohydrates; 0 Cholesterol; 596mg Sodium; 6g Fiber

Jicama and Potato Salad

Crisp jicama adds a moist crunchiness to this quick-and-easy potato salad.

4 cups peeled and diced white potatoes
2 tablespoons canola oil
2 tablespoons rice vinegar
1 tablespoon Dijon-style mustard
2 tablespoons chopped cilantro
½ teaspoon salt
½ teaspoon freshly ground black pepper
1 cup peeled and diced jicama
½ cup jarred roasted red peppers, diced
4 whole scallions, trimmed and chopped

In a medium saucepan, place the potatoes in boiling water to cover and cook until easily pierced with a fork, about 15 minutes. Drain and cool slightly under cold running water.

In a mixing bowl, whisk together the oil, vinegar, mustard, cilantro, salt, and pepper. Blend in the potatoes, jicama, bell peppers, and scallions. Chill for 15 to 30 minutes before serving.

Makes six 1-cup servings

Per serving:
296 Calories; 6g Protein; 7g Fat;
54g Carbohydrates; 0 Cholesterol;
327mg Sodium; 6g Fiber

Two-Bean and Avocado Salad with Jicama

Jicama, also called Mexican potato, offers a crisp, celerylike crunch to this sprightly bean salad. Unlike a potato, jicama is typically eaten raw.

One 15-ounce can black beans, drained
One 15-ounce can red kidney beans, drained
2 tomatoes, diced
1 ripe avocado, peeled, pitted, and diced (see Helpful Hints, page 11)
1 cup peeled and diced jicama
4 whole scallions, trimmed and chopped
2 cloves garlic, minced
Juice of 1 lime
2 tablespoons chopped cilantro
1 tablespoon canola oil
2 teaspoons dried oregano
1 teaspoon ground cumin
½ teaspoon salt
½ teaspoon freshly ground black pepper

Combine all of the ingredients in a mixing bowl and blend thoroughly. Chill for 15 to 30 minutes before serving.

To serve, spoon the salad over a bed of leaf lettuce.

Makes 6 servings

Per serving:
189 Calories; 7g Protein; 7g Fat; 28g Carbohydrates; 0 Cholesterol; 680mg Sodium; 12g Fiber

CHAPTER 3

Main Dishes

Vegetable Posole

This meatless cousin of Tex-Mex chili is a hearty cauldron of vegetables, beans, and assertive spices.

1 tablespoon canola oil
1 medium yellow onion, diced
1 large red or green bell pepper, seeded and diced
2 cloves garlic, minced
One 28-ounce can crushed tomatoes
One 15-ounce can hominy corn, drained
One 15-ounce can red kidney beans, drained
One 14-ounce can stewed tomatoes, undrained
½ cup water
1 tablespoon dried oregano
1 tablespoon chili powder
2 teaspoons ground cumin
½ teaspoon salt
½ teaspoon freshly ground black pepper

In a large saucepan, heat the oil over medium heat. Add the onion, bell pepper, and garlic and cook, stirring, until tender, about 5 minutes. Stir in the remaining ingredients and bring to a simmer. Reduce heat to medium-low and cook about 20 minutes, stirring occasionally.

Remove from the heat and let stand for 5 minutes before serving. Offer warm flour tortillas on the side.

Makes 6 servings

Per serving:
198 Calories; 6g Protein; 5g Fat; 32g Carbohydrates; 0 Cholesterol; 1,306mg Sodium; 8g Fiber

Wild Mushroom Burritos

This "gourmet wrap" is filled with a medley of mushrooms, beans, corn, and bell peppers.

1 tablespoon canola oil
4 ounces fresh shiitake
    mushrooms, sliced
4 ounces fresh oyster or
    cremini mushrooms,
    sliced
4 ounces fresh white mush-
    rooms, sliced
1 red bell pepper, seeded and
    diced
2 large cloves garlic, minced
One 15-ounce can black beans
    or red kidney beans,
    drained
One 14-ounce can corn kernels,
    drained
4 whole scallions, trimmed
    and chopped
1 teaspoon ground cumin
Six 10-inch flour tortillas
¾ cup shredded low-fat
    Monterey Jack cheese
About 1 cup tomato salsa

In a medium saucepan or large nonstick skillet, heat the oil over medium heat. Add the mushrooms, bell pepper, and garlic and cook, stirring, until tender, about 7 minutes. Stir in the beans, corn, scallions, and cumin and cook, stirring, 4 to 6 minutes.

Meanwhile, warm the flour tortillas over a hot burner or skillet and place on large serving plates. Spoon the mushroom mixture down the center of each tortilla. Top each filling with about 2 tablespoons of cheese; roll the tortillas around the fillings, creating burritos. Spoon your favorite salsa over the top of each burrito. Serve with rice on the side.

**Makes 6 burritos
(6 servings)**

Per serving:
307 Calories; 15g Protein; 8g Fat;
51g Carbohydrates; 10mg Cholesterol; 939mg Sodium; 8g Fiber

Macaroni Con Queso

*Pure comfort food, this version of macaroni
and cheese has a Mexican twist.*

1 cup elbow macaroni
2 teaspoons canola oil
1 medium yellow onion, diced
**1 green bell pepper, seeded
and diced**
4 cloves garlic, minced
**One 28-ounce can stewed
tomatoes, undrained**
**One 15-ounce can pinto beans
or black beans, drained**
**One 11-ounce can corn kernels,
drained**
1 tablespoon chili powder
2 teaspoons dried oregano
1 teaspoon ground cumin
½ teaspoon salt
**½ teaspoon freshly ground
black pepper**
**½ cup shredded low-fat
Monterey Jack cheese**

In a medium saucepan, bring
2½ quarts of water to a boil over
medium-high heat. Place the
macaroni in the boiling water, stir,
and return to a boil. Cook until
al dente, about 6 minutes, stirring
occasionally. Drain in a colander.

Meanwhile, in a large saucepan,
heat the oil over medium-high
heat. Add the onion, bell pepper,
and garlic and cook, stirring, until
the onion is translucent, about
5 minutes. Stir in the stewed
tomatoes and juice, beans, corn,
chili powder, oregano, cumin, salt,
and pepper and bring to a simmer.
Cook over medium-low heat for
15 minutes, stirring occasionally.
Fold in the cooked macaroni and
cook for 3 to 4 minutes over low
heat. Remove from the heat and
fold in the cheese. Let stand for
5 minutes before serving.

Ladle into wide bowls and
serve with warm flour tortillas.

Makes 6 servings

Per serving:
251 Calories; 8g Protein; 3g Fat;
45g Carbohydrates; 4mg Cholesterol; 244mg Sodium; 9g Fiber

Quesadillas with Pinto Beans and Corn

Dinner doesn't get much easier than this.

One 15-ounce can corn kernels, drained
One 15-ounce can pinto beans, drained
2 whole scallions, trimmed and chopped
2 tablespoons chopped cilantro
½ teaspoon salt
½ teaspoon freshly ground black pepper
¼ cup shredded low-fat provolone or Monterey Jack cheese
Eight 6-inch flour tortillas
About 1 cup taco sauce or tomato salsa

Preheat the oven to 400°F.

In a mixing bowl, combine the corn, beans, scallions, cilantro, salt, pepper, and cheese. Arrange the tortillas on two large baking pans. Spread about ½ cup of the bean and corn mixture over one-half of each of the tortillas. Fold over the remaining sides. Bake until the tortillas are lightly browned, 6 to 8 minutes.

Using a wide spatula, transfer the quesadillas to serving plates. Spoon the taco sauce or salsa over the tops and serve at once.

**Makes 8 quesadillas
(4 servings)**

Per serving:
230 Calories; 8g Protein; 3g Fat; 42g Carbohydrates; 2mg Cholesterol; 866mg Sodium; 5g Fiber

Red Pepper and Corn Polenta

This wholesome dish of cornmeal porridge makes a hearty accompaniment to grilled or roasted vegetables. And polenta sounds so much better than cornmeal gruel or corn mush, which are other names for the savory dish.

3 cups water
1 cup yellow cornmeal
½ teaspoon salt
**½ teaspoon freshly ground
   black pepper**
**One 11-ounce can corn kernels,
   drained**
**½ cup jarred roasted red
   peppers, diced**
**¼ cup grated Parmesan cheese
   or shredded Monterey Jack
   cheese**
1 cup tomato salsa (optional)

In a sturdy, heavy-bottomed saucepan, add the water and bring to a boil over medium-high heat. Reduce the heat to low and gradually stir in the cornmeal, salt, and black pepper. Cook, stirring frequently, until the mixture thickens and most lumps disappear, 12 to 14 minutes. (A wooden spoon should be able to stand up straight in the center of the pot.) Fold in the corn, roasted peppers, and cheese and cook, stirring, for 1 minute. Remove the pan from the heat.

Spoon the polenta onto plates. If desired, top with salsa.

Makes 6 servings

Per serving:
144 Calories; 5g Protein; 2g Fat; 27g Carbohydrates; 3mg Cholesterol; 632mg Sodium; 4g Fiber

Vegetable Burritos with Roasted Pepper Pesto

*An intensely fragrant pesto sauce imbues this
burrito with arresting herbal flavors.*

**2 cups fresh basil leaves,
  coarsely chopped**
**½ cup jarred roasted red
  peppers**
1 tomato, chopped
3 to 4 cloves garlic
**¼ cup coarsely chopped
  walnuts**
**2 tablespoons plus 2 teaspoons
  canola oil**
**¼ cup grated Parmesan cheese
  (optional)**
**2 green or red bell peppers,
  seeded and diced**
1 medium zucchini, diced
**8 ounces fresh white mush-
  rooms, sliced**
**One 14-ounce can corn kernels,
  drained**
Six 10-inch flour tortillas

Add the basil, bell peppers,
tomato, garlic, walnuts, and 2
tablespoons oil to a blender or
food processor fitted with a steel
blade and process about 5 seconds. Stop to scrape the sides and
continue processing until smooth,
about 5 seconds. Transfer to a
mixing bowl. If desired, blend in
the cheese.

In a large saucepan, heat the
remaining 2 teaspoons oil over
medium-high heat. Add the bell
peppers, zucchini, and mushrooms and cook, stirring, until
tender, about 7 minutes. Stir in
the corn and cook, stirring, for
4 minutes. Remove from the heat
and blend in the pesto sauce.

Warm the flour tortillas over a
hot burner or skillet and place on
serving plates. Spoon the vegetable mixture down the center of
each tortilla and roll the tortillas
around the filling, creating burritos. Serve with rice and salsa on
the side.

**Makes 6 burritos
(6 servings)**

Per serving:
281 Calories; 9g Protein; 10g Fat;
42g Carbohydrates; 0 Cholesterol;
533mg Sodium; 13g Fiber

Mexican Beer Chili

A true beer-lover's chili.

1 tablespoon canola oil
1 medium yellow onion, diced
1 green bell pepper, seeded
    and diced
1 large rib celery, chopped
2 large cloves garlic, minced
One 15-ounce can black beans,
    undrained
One 15-ounce can red kidney
    beans, undrained
One 14-ounce can stewed
    tomatoes, undrained
½ cup flat Mexican beer, such
    as Dos Equis® or Corona®
½ cup water
1 white potato, peeled and
    diced
1 tablespoon dried oregano
1 tablespoon chili powder
1 teaspoon ground cumin
½ teaspoon salt
½ teaspoon freshly ground
    black pepper

In a large saucepan, heat the oil over medium heat. Add the onion, bell pepper, celery, and garlic and cook, stirring, until tender, about 5 minutes. Add the remaining ingredients and bring to a simmer. Cook over medium heat until the potato is tender, about 20 minutes, stirring occasionally.

Ladle the chili into bowls and serve at once.

Makes 4 servings

VARIATIONS

Offer a topping for the chili, such as low-fat plain yogurt or shredded cheese.

Per serving:
265 Calories; 12g Protein; 4g Fat; 49g Carbohydrates; 0 Cholesterol; 1,256mg Sodium; 14g Fiber

"TVP" Tacos with Soft Corn Tortillas

TVP, otherwise known as textured vegetable protein, may sound intimidating, but it makes the perfect meat substitute in recipes for tacos, tostadas, and chili.

1 tablespoon canola oil
1 small onion, chopped
4 ounces fresh white
    mushrooms, sliced
1 cup water
1 cup TVP, mince-style
2 tablespoons commercial
    taco seasoning (see
    Helpful Hint, page 19)
2 tomatoes, diced
1 small head romaine lettuce,
    cut into ribbons
1 cup low-fat plain yogurt
1 cup taco sauce
Six 6-inch soft corn tortillas

In a medium saucepan, heat the oil over medium heat. Add the onion and mushrooms and cook, stirring, until tender, about 5 minutes. Add the water, TVP, and taco seasoning and bring to a simmer. Cook, stirring, for 8 to 10 minutes. Transfer the mixture to a warm serving bowl.

Meanwhile, arrange the tomatoes, lettuce, yogurt, and taco sauce in individual serving bowls. Warm the corn tortillas over a hot burner or skillet and stack on large serving plates. To serve, spoon about ¼ cup of the vegetable-TVP mixture onto the center of each taco and top with the diced tomatoes, yogurt, lettuce, and taco sauce. Fold the tacos around the filling; serve with plenty of napkins.

**Makes 6 tacos
(3 servings)**

Per serving:
398 Calories; 34g Protein; 8g Fat; 56g Carbohydrates; 4mg Cholesterol; 1,341mg Sodium; 12g Fiber

Mayan Vegetable Pepper Pot

The fiery habanero, considered to be the world's hottest pepper, has been cultivated for centuries in the Yucatán—long before Columbus arrived. Thus, a penchant for pungent food can be traced way back to the ancient Mayan civilization.

1 tablespoon canola oil
1 medium yellow onion, diced
1 green bell pepper, seeded
**   and diced**
1 orange habanero pepper,
**   seeded and minced**
4 cups coarsely chopped fresh
**   spinach**
3 cups vegetable broth
1 white potato, diced
1 chayote, seeded and diced
**   (see Helpful Hints)**
2 teaspoons dried oregano
1 teaspoon ground cumin
½ teaspoon salt
14-ounce can stewed tomatoes,
**   undrained**
2 tablespoons masa harina
**   (see Helpful Hints)**
4 cups cooked white rice or
**   quinoa (see Helpful Hints)**

In a large saucepan, heat the oil over medium heat. Add the onion, bell pepper, and habanero pepper and cook, stirring, until the onion is translucent, about 5 minutes. Add the spinach and cook until wilted, about 2 minutes. Add the vegetable broth, potato, chayote, oregano, cumin, and salt and bring to a simmer. Cook over medium heat for 10 minutes, stirring occasionally. Stir in the stewed tomatoes and liquid and continue cooking until the potato and chayote are tender, stirring occasionally, about another 10 minutes. Gradually whisk the masa harina into the pepper pot and stir until most of the lumps disappear. Cook for 5 to 10 minutes over low heat. Let stand for 5 minutes before serving.

Spoon the rice into wide bowls and ladle the pepper pot over the top. Serve at once with a cooling beverage—this meal has a spicy kick to it.

Makes 6 servings

Per serving:
249 Calories; 7g Protein; 3g Fat; 49g Carbohydrates; 0 Cholesterol; 905mg Sodium; 3g Fiber

Helpful Hints

Although best known for its role in tamales and corn tortillas, masa harina, a superfine corn flour, can also be used like cornstarch to thicken stews and sauces.

For 4 cups of cooked rice, combine about 1½ cups uncooked rice with 3 cups water and cook until tender.

Chayote is a pear-shaped Mexican squash with a pale green skin and creamy white flesh. Like zucchini, almost the whole chayote can be shredded. There are a few large seeds in the center, which should be removed.

Sofrito Rice and Beans

Sofrito *refers to an aromatic mixture of tomatoes, onion, peppers, and garlic.* Sofrito *makes a perfect base for this quick-and-easy rice dish.*

1 tablespoon canola oil
1 medium yellow onion, diced
1 green bell pepper, seeded
    and diced
3 to 4 cloves garlic, minced
One 14-ounce can stewed
    tomatoes, drained
3 cups water
1½ cups long-grain white rice
    or brown rice
One 15-ounce can red kidney
    beans, drained
1 tablespoon chopped pickled
    jalapeños
2 teaspoons dried oregano
1 teaspoon salt
½ teaspoon freshly ground
    black pepper

In a medium saucepan, heat the oil over medium heat. Add the onion, bell pepper, and garlic and cook, stirring, until tender, 5 to 6 minutes. Stir in remaining ingredients and bring to a simmer. Cover and cook over medium-low heat until all of the liquid is absorbed, about 20 minutes. Fluff the rice with a fork and let stand, covered, about 5 minutes before serving.

Makes 6 servings

VARIATION

If using fresh jalapeño instead of pickled, add 1 large green chili, seeded and minced.

Per serving:
211 Calories; 6g Protein; 3g Fat;
40g Carbohydrates; 0 Cholesterol;
753mg Sodium; 6g Fiber

Spinach and Mushroom Enchiladas

*Spinach and mushrooms share a natural affinity for each other.
A touch of cheddar cheese adds a lively boost of flavor.*

2½ cups water
1¼ cups long-grain white rice
    or basmati rice
1 tablespoon canola oil
2 tablespoons dry white wine
1 pound fresh white mush-
    rooms, sliced
1 medium yellow onion, diced
2 cloves garlic, minced
6 cups coarsely chopped
    fresh spinach
½ teaspoon salt
½ teaspoon freshly ground
    black pepper
Six 10-inch flour tortillas
One 10-ounce can enchilada
    sauce (1¼ cups)
½ cup shredded low-fat
    cheddar cheese

Preheat the oven to 375°F.

In a medium saucepan, combine the water and rice and bring to simmer over medium-high heat. Stir the rice, cover the pan, and cook over medium-low heat until all of the liquid is absorbed, about 15 minutes. Fluff the grains with a fork and let stand, covered, for 5 minutes.

Meanwhile, in a large saucepan, heat the oil and wine. Add the mushrooms, onion, and garlic and cook, stirring, over medium heat until the mushrooms are moist and tender, about 7 minutes. Stir in the spinach, salt, and pepper and cook until the greens are wilted, about 4 minutes, stirring occasionally. Fold in the rice.

Place a tortilla on a flat surface and spoon 1 heaping cup of the spinach-rice mixture down the center. Wrap the tortilla around the filling and place in a large, lightly greased casserole or 9×13-inch baking pan. Continue filling the remaining tortillas and arrange side by side in the casserole dish. Drizzle the enchilada sauce over the top and sprinkle with shredded cheese. Place in the oven and bake until the cheese melts, about 5 minutes. Remove from the heat and serve at once.

**Makes 6 enchiladas
(6 servings)**

Per serving:
351 Calories; 11g Protein; 7g Fat;
58g Carbohydrates; 10mg Cholesterol; 983mg Sodium; 8g Fiber

Succotash Burrito

The classic duet of lima beans and corn
give this burrito an appealing twist.

1 tablespoon canola oil
1 medium zucchini, diced
1 red bell pepper, seeded
   and diced
8 ounces fresh white mushrooms, sliced
2 cloves garlic, minced
2 cups frozen lima beans
One 15-ounce can corn kernels,
   drained
½ teaspoon salt
½ teaspoon freshly ground
   black pepper
Four 10-inch flour tortillas
¼ cup shredded low-fat Swiss
   cheese
1 cup prepared tomato salsa

In a medium saucepan or large nonstick skillet, heat the oil over medium heat. Add the zucchini, bell pepper, mushrooms, and garlic and cook, stirring frequently, until tender, about 7 minutes. Stir in the lima beans, corn, salt, and pepper and cook, stirring, until the mixture is steaming, 8 to 10 minutes.

Warm the flour tortillas over a hot burner or skillet and place on large serving plates. Spoon the vegetable mixture down the center of each tortilla. Top each with about 1 tablespoon of cheese. Roll the tortillas around the filling, forming burritos. Spoon the salsa over the top of each burrito and serve at once.

Makes 4 burritos
(4 servings)

Per serving:
378 Calories; 19g Protein; 9g Fat;
64g Carbohydrates; 5mg Cholesterol; 1,182mg Sodium; 6g Fiber

Pasta with Pumpkin Seed Pesto

*Toasted pumpkin seeds add an earthy, nutty undertone to pesto sauce. Be
sure to use raw pumpkin seeds (typically, dark green), not commercially
roasted and salted pumpkin seeds (white seeds intended for snacking).*

½ cup raw pumpkin seeds
(see Helpful Hint, page 13)
4 cloves garlic, chopped
2 tomatoes, chopped
1 cup packed spinach leaves
1 cup packed fresh basil leaves
2 to 3 tablespoons olive oil
½ teaspoon salt
½ teaspoon freshly ground
black pepper
¼ cup freshly grated Parmesan
cheese
12 ounces penne or ziti

Add the seeds to a hot, ungreased
skillet. Cook, stirring, over medium heat until the seeds are lightly
toasted and popping like popcorn,
about 3 minutes. Remove from the
heat and set aside.

Add the seeds, garlic, tomatoes,
spinach, basil, oil, salt, and pepper to a blender or food processor
fitted with a steel blade. Process
for about 5 seconds; stop to scrape
the sides. Process for an additional

5 seconds; stop again to scrape the
sides. Continue processing until
the mixture is smooth, about
10 seconds more. Transfer to a
medium bowl and fold in the
cheese.

Meanwhile, in a large saucepan,
bring 2½ quarts of water to a boil
over medium-high heat. Place the
pasta in the boiling water, stir,
and return to a boil. Cook over
medium-high heat until *al dente,*
9 to 11 minutes, stirring occasionally. Drain in a colander.

Toss the pasta with the pesto
sauce and serve at once.

Makes 4 servings

VARIATIONS

*A variety of ingredients can
be added to the pasta such
as artichokes, corn, blanched
asparagus, chickpeas, or roasted
red peppers.*

Per serving:
310 Calories; 12g Protein; 17g Fat;
29g Carbohydrates; 32mg Cholesterol; 410mg Sodium; 3g Fiber

Ancho Vegetable Stew

Ancho chilies (dried poblanos) have a raisiny flavor and medium heat level.

**2 to 3 dried ancho chilies,
  seeded**
1 cup simmering water
1 tablespoon canola oil
1 large yellow onion, diced
**1 red bell pepper, seeded
  and diced**
1 medium zucchini, diced
2 large cloves garlic, minced
**One 14-ounce can stewed
  tomatoes, undrained**
4 cups water
**1 large white potato, peeled
  and diced**
**One 11-ounce can corn kernels,
  drained**
1 tablespoon dried parsley
2 teaspoons dried oregano
1½ teaspoons ground cumin
1 teaspoon salt
¼ cup tomato paste

Add the chilies to an ungreased skillet. Cook over medium heat until lightly toasted, about 2 minutes, occasionally shaking the pan and turning the chilies as they cook. Remove from the heat. In a large mixing bowl, cover the chilies with the simmering water. Place a lid or plate over the chilies to keep them from floating, and soak for 20 minutes.

Add the chilies and about ½ cup of the soaking liquid to a blender and puree, about 5 seconds. Scrape into a small bowl; set aside.

Meanwhile, in a large saucepan, heat the oil over medium heat. Add the onion, bell pepper, zucchini, and garlic and cook, stirring, until tender, about 6 minutes. Stir in the remaining ingredients except tomato paste and pureed chilies and bring to a simmer. Reduce heat to medium-low and cook, stirring occasionally, until the potatoes are tender, about 20 minutes. Stir in the tomato paste and pureed chilies and cook for 5 minutes.

Let the stew stand for 5 to 10 minutes before serving. Ladle into bowls and serve with warm flour tortillas.

Makes 8 servings

VARIATION

To make this stew into a full course meal, add one 15-ounce can of drained red kidney beans to the simmering pot.

Per serving:
98 Calories; 3g Protein; 2g Fat; 18g Carbohydrates; 0 Cholesterol; 555mg Sodium; 3g Fiber

Roasted Peppers with Couscous and Chickpeas

2¼ cups boiling water

1½ cups couscous

One 15-ounce can chickpeas, drained

½ cup chopped parsley

½ teaspoon salt

½ teaspoon freshly ground black pepper

6 large poblano chilies or green bell peppers

1 cup tomato salsa

¾ cup low-fat plain yogurt

Preheat the oven to 400°F.

Combine the boiling water, couscous, chickpeas, parsley, salt, and pepper in a bowl and cover. Let stand for 10 minutes. Fluff the grains with a fork and let stand, covered.

Meanwhile, slit the poblanos in half lengthwise and remove the seeds. Arrange in a casserole dish or baking pan and bake until the peppers are tender and the outer skin is bubbly, 15 to 20 minutes. Remove from the oven and place on serving plates. Fill each pod with the couscous mixture. Spoon the salsa and yogurt over the top and serve at once.

Makes 6 servings

Per serving:
296 Calories; 11g Protein; 1g Fat; 59g Carbohydrates; 2mg Cholesterol; 703mg Sodium; 6g Fiber

Calabacita Vegetable Burritos

The term calabacitas *not only refers to a variety of summer squash, it can also describe a medley of vegetables, as it does here.*

1 tablespoon canola oil
8 ounces fresh white mushrooms, sliced
1 medium zucchini, diced
1 red bell pepper, seeded
  and diced
2 large cloves garlic, minced
One 15-ounce can black beans
  or red kidney beans,
  drained
One 11-ounce can corn kernels,
  drained
4 whole scallions, trimmed
  and chopped
1 teaspoon ground cumin
Four 10-inch flour tortillas
1 cup shredded low-fat
  Monterey Jack cheese
  (optional)
About 1 cup prepared tomato
  salsa

In a medium saucepan or large nonstick skillet, heat the oil over medium heat. Add the mushrooms, zucchini, bell pepper, and garlic and cook, stirring frequently, until tender, about 7 minutes. Stir in the beans, corn, scallions, and cumin and cook, stirring frequently, until the mixture is steaming, about 6 minutes.

Warm the flour tortillas over a hot burner or skillet and place on large serving plates. Spoon the vegetable mixture down the center of each tortilla. If desired, top each with about 2 tablespoons of cheese. Roll the tortillas around the fillings, forming burritos. Spoon your favorite salsa over the top of each burrito. Rice is the traditional accompaniment.

**Makes 4 burritos
(4 servings)**

Per serving:
314 Calories; 15g Protein; 7g Fat;
60g Carbohydrates; 0 Cholesterol;
1,249mg Sodium; 10g Fiber

Seitan Torta

Tortas are large, overstuffed sandwiches filled with a variety of toppings, sort of a Mexican version of hoagies or po'boys. Chewy, thinly sliced seitan makes a natural substitute for the traditional meat filling.

One 16-ounce can refried black beans
Four 7-inch crusty French bread rolls
8 ounces seitan (see Helpful Hint), thinly sliced
1 cup tomato salsa
½ cup shredded Monterey Jack cheese
8 leaves romaine lettuce, shredded
1 medium red onion, thinly sliced

Preheat the broiler.

Add the refried beans to a medium saucepan. Cook, stirring, over medium heat until the beans are steaming, 4 to 5 minutes. Set aside.

Slice the rolls in half lengthwise and arrange on a baking pan cut-side up. Spread 2 to 3 tablespoons of refried beans over half of each roll. Cover the beans with the seitan. Top with the salsa and cheese. Place the rolls beneath the broiler and broil until the cheese melts and the sides are toasted, about 2 minutes. Remove from the oven and transfer to a serving platter.

Fill each sandwich with shredded romaine and onion. Fold the rolls into sandwiches and serve at once.

Makes 4 sandwiches (4 servings)

VARIATIONS

Other vegetarian fillings can include sliced avocados, scallions, chili rajas, or roasted red peppers.

Helpful Hint

Seitan, sometimes called gluten or "wheat meat," is a chewy, meatlike food made from wheat gluten and water. The gluten dough is simmered in a flavored broth, then sliced, chunked, or ground, depending on how it will be used. Its chewy texture makes it a perfect meat substitute. It can be made from whole wheat flour or from a mix. It can also be purchased ready-made.

Per serving:
468 Calories; 36g Protein; 7g Fat; 66g Carbohydrates; 15mg Cholesterol; 1,480mg Sodium; 7g Fiber

Black Bean Empanadas

*Empanadas are savory pockets of dough stuffed with a variety
of fillings. Like calzones and falafel pitas, empanadas
can be eaten out of hand or on the run.*

One 15-ounce can black beans
1 tablespoon canola oil
1 medium yellow onion, diced
1 teaspoon dried oregano
1 teaspoon ground cumin
½ teaspoon salt
**½ teaspoon freshly ground
    black pepper**
**1 pound frozen bread dough or
    pizza dough, thawed in the
    refrigerator**
Salsa or guacamole (optional)

Preheat the oven to 375°F. Drain
the beans, reserving ¼ cup of the
liquid.

In a medium saucepan, heat the
oil over medium heat. Add the
onion and cook, stirring, until
tender, about 4 minutes. Add the
black beans, bean liquid, oregano,
cumin, salt, and pepper and cook
for 6 to 7 minutes. Reduce heat to
low, then transfer three-quarters
of the bean mixture to a blender
or a food processor fitted with
a steel blade and process until
smooth, about 5 seconds, stopping
to stir at least once. Return the
bean mixture to the pan and cook,
stirring frequently, for 5 minutes.
Let cool slightly.

On a flat work surface, form
the dough into 6 equal-size balls.
Roll each ball into a flat circle.
Fill the center of each round
with 3 to 4 tablespoons of the
pureed beans. Fold the dough
over the filling and seal the
edges with the back of a fork,
forming empanadas. Place
the empanadas onto a lightly
greased baking sheet and bake
until golden brown, about 15
minutes. Let empanadas cool for
a few minutes before serving. If
desired, serve salsa or guacamole
as a condiment.

**Makes 6 empanadas
(6 servings)**

Per serving:
328 Calories; 11g Protein; 6g Fat;
63g Carbohydrates; 0 Cholesterol;
819mg Sodium; 5g Fiber

Tempeh Chili Burritos

*Chewy tempeh combines with tomatoes, beans, and chili seasonings
to create a hearty and robust burrito filling.*

1 tablespoon canola oil
1 yellow onion, diced
1 green bell pepper, seeded
 and diced
2 ribs celery, chopped
One 28-ounce can crushed
 tomatoes
¼ cup water
One 15-ounce can red kidney
 beans, drained
8 ounces tempeh, diced
1 tablespoon chili powder
1 tablespoon commercial taco
 seasoning (see Helpful
 Hint, page 19)
½ teaspoon salt
½ teaspoon freshly ground
 black pepper
Six 10-inch flour tortillas
½ cup low-fat plain yogurt
 (optional)

In a large saucepan, heat the oil
over medium heat. Add the onion,
bell pepper, and celery and cook,
stirring, until tender, about
6 minutes. Stir in the crushed
tomatoes, water, beans, tempeh,
chili powder, taco seasoning, salt,
and pepper and bring to a simmer.
Reduce heat to medium-low and
cook, stirring occasionally, for
15 minutes. Remove from the heat
and let stand for 5 minutes.

Meanwhile, warm the flour
tortillas over a hot burner or
skillet and place on serving plates.
Spoon the tempeh-chili down the
center of each tortilla. Roll the
tortillas around the fillings, creating burritos. If desired, serve
yogurt as a condiment. Rice makes
a complementary side dish.

**Makes 6 burritos
(6 servings)**

Per serving:
282 Calories; 16g Protein; 6g Fat;
44g Carbohydrates; 0 Cholesterol;
831mg Sodium; 17g Fiber

Mexican Jambalaya

*Corn, jalapeños, and nopalitos (small cactus paddles)
give this satisfying jambalaya a Mexican accent.*

3½ **cups water**
1¼ **cups white rice**
1 **tablespoon canola oil**
8 **ounces fresh white mush-
    rooms, sliced**
1 **medium yellow onion, diced**
1 **green bell pepper, diced**
1 **medium zucchini, diced**
½ **cup tomato paste**
**One 11-ounce can corn kernels,
    drained**
1 **cup jarred nopalitos, rinsed
    and cut into strips (see
    Helpful Hint)**
1 **tablespoon minced pickled
    jalapeños**
2 **teaspoons dried oregano**
1 **teaspoon ground cumin**
½ **teaspoon salt**
½ **teaspoon freshly ground
    black pepper**

In a medium saucepan, combine
2½ cups water and the rice and
bring to a simmer over medium-
high heat. Stir the rice, cover the
pan, and cook over medium-low
heat until all of the liquid is
absorbed, about 15 minutes. Fluff
the grains with a fork and let
stand, still covered, for 5 minutes.

In another medium saucepan
heat the oil over medium heat.

Add the mushrooms, onion, bell
pepper, and zucchini, and cook,
stirring, until the vegetables are
tender, about 7 minutes. Stir in
the remaining 1 cup water and
tomato paste, creating a sauce.
Add the remaining ingredients
and bring to a simmer. Cook 5 to
7 minutes over medium heat,
stirring occasionally. Fold in the
cooked rice. Ladle the jambalaya
onto plates and serve with warm
flour tortillas.

Makes 4 servings

VARIATION

*About ¼ cup steamed green beans
can be substituted for the nopalitos.*

Helpful Hint

*There seems to be a consensus to
purchase nopalitos in see-through
jars as opposed to cans, which may
hide the quality of the cactus.*

Per serving:
377 Calories; 10g Protein; 5g Fat;
73g Carbohydrates; 0 Cholesterol;
324mg Sodium; 7g Fiber

Quintessential Bean Quesadillas

Low-fat yogurt replaces the traditional sour cream in these quick-and-easy quesadillas. Homemade refried beans make a simple but satisfying filling.

Two 15-ounce cans pinto beans
1 tablespoon canola oil
1 medium yellow onion, diced
2 cloves garlic, minced
1 tablespoon chopped pickled jalapeños
2 teaspoons dried oregano
½ teaspoon salt
½ teaspoon freshly ground black pepper
Six 7-inch flour tortillas
2 tomatoes, diced
4 whole scallions, trimmed and chopped
½ to ¾ cup low-fat plain yogurt

Drain the canned beans, reserving ½ cup of the liquid.

In a medium saucepan, heat the oil over medium-high heat. Add the onion and garlic and cook, stirring frequently, until tender, about 4 minutes. Add the beans, bean liquid, jalapeños, oregano, salt, and pepper; reduce heat to medium-low and cook, stirring frequently, until beans are heated through, about 8 minutes.

Transfer the bean mixture to a blender or a food processor fitted with a steel blade and process until smooth, about 5 seconds, stopping to stir at least once. Return the puree to the pan and cook over low heat, stirring, about 5 minutes.

Meanwhile, warm the flour tortillas over a hot burner or skillet and place on serving plates. Spoon about ⅓ cup of the bean mixture over one-half of each tortilla. Top the beans with the tomatoes, scallions, and 1 to 2 tablespoons yogurt. Fold the remaining half of the tortilla over the filling.

**Makes 6 quesadillas
(6 servings)**

Per serving:
281 Calories, 9g Protein; 6g Fat; 47g Carbohydrates; 1mg Cholesterol; 938mg Sodium; 6g Fiber

California "Wraps" with Artichokes and Goat Cheese

*In California, the humble burrito has evolved into a trendy gourmet
"wrap," into which anything goes. Artichokes, tofu, and goat
cheese are some of the more popular fillings.*

1 tablespoon canola oil
1 medium zucchini, diced
1 red bell pepper, seeded
   and diced
8 ounces fresh white mushrooms, sliced
2 cloves garlic, minced
One 15-ounce can artichoke
   hearts, drained and
   coarsely chopped
4 ounces extra-firm tofu, diced
1 teaspoon dried basil
½ teaspoon salt
½ teaspoon freshly ground
   black pepper
Four 10-inch flour tortillas
4 ounces chèvre (smooth
   goat cheese)
1 cup tomato salsa or
   guacamole

In a medium saucepan or large
nonstick skillet, heat the oil over
medium heat. Add the zucchini,
bell pepper, mushrooms, and
garlic and cook, stirring, until
tender, about 6 minutes. Stir in
the artichokes, tofu, basil, salt,
and pepper and cook, stirring,
until the mixture is steaming,
about 4 minutes.

Warm the flour tortillas over
a hot burner or skillet and place
on large serving plates. Spread
about 1 tablespoon of chèvre over
the top of each tortilla. Spoon
the vegetable mixture down the
center of the tortillas. Roll the
tortillas around the filling and
enclose the ends, forming a
package. Serve salsa with each
wrap.

**Makes 4 wraps
(4 servings)**

Per serving:
317 Calories; 14g Protein; 10g Fat;
45g Carbohydrates; 6mg Cholesterol; 1,356mg Sodium; 6g Fiber

Tomatillo Posole

*Tomatillos are quite similar to green tomatoes in appearance and texture.
They add a mildly tart flavor to this tomato-based hominy stew.*

1 tablespoon canola oil
1 medium yellow onion, diced
1 green bell pepper, seeded
  and diced
2 ribs celery, chopped
2 cloves garlic, minced
1 to 2 tablespoons chopped
  pickled jalapeños
One 15-ounce can crushed
  tomatoes
One 14-ounce can stewed
  tomatoes, undrained
One 14-ounce can hominy corn
  or corn kernels, drained
One 12-ounce can tomatillos,
  drained and diced
1 tablespoon chili powder
1 tablespoon dried oregano
½ teaspoon salt
½ teaspoon freshly ground
  black pepper

In a large saucepan, heat the oil
over medium-high heat. Add the
onion, bell pepper, celery, garlic,
and jalapeños and cook, stirring,
until tender, 5 to 7 minutes. Stir
in the remaining ingredients and
bring to a simmer. Reduce heat
to medium-low and cook for
15 minutes, stirring occasionally.
Remove from the heat and
let stand for 5 minutes before
serving.

Ladle the *posole* into bowls and
serve with warm flour tortillas or
corn bread.

Makes 4 servings

Per serving:
194 Calories; 5g Protein; 5g Fat;
33g Carbohydrates; 0 Cholesterol;
891mg Sodium; 7g Fiber

Eggplant and Red Bean Chilaquiles

This baked tortilla dish is a down-home casserole
of eggplant, tomatoes, and beans.

1 tablespoon canola oil
1 medium yellow onion, diced
1 green bell pepper, seeded
    and minced
2 cloves garlic, minced
One 28-ounce can plum
    tomatoes, undrained
2 cups diced eggplant
2 teaspoons dried oregano
1 teaspoon ground cumin
½ teaspoon salt
½ teaspoon freshly ground
    black pepper
One 15-ounce can red kidney
    beans, drained
Eight 6-inch soft corn tortillas,
    torn into wide strips
½ cup shredded low-fat
    Monterey Jack or Swiss
    cheese

Preheat the oven to 375°F.

In a large saucepan, heat the oil over medium heat. Add the onion, bell pepper, and garlic and cook, stirring, until tender, about 5 minutes. Add the plum tomatoes and juice, eggplant, oregano, cumin, salt, and pepper and bring to a simmer. Cook until eggplant is tender, stirring occasionally, 12 to 15 minutes. Cut the tomatoes into smaller pieces as the stew cooks. Stir in the beans during last 5 minutes.

Place a layer of tortilla strips on the bottom of two 9-inch pie pans. Cover each pan with about one-quarter of the eggplant mixture and 2 to 3 tablespoons cheese. Form another layer of tortilla strips; follow again with the eggplant mixture and cheese. Bake until the cheese is bubbly, about 10 minutes. Remove from the oven and let stand for 5 minutes before serving.

Makes 6 to 8 servings

Per serving:
236 Calories; 11g Protein; 5g Fat; 37g Carbohydrates; 7mg Cholesterol; 849mg Sodium; 9g Fiber

Tamale Bean Pie

Masa harina—the ultra-fine corn flour used to make tamales and corn tortillas—is also used to form the crust for these savory bean pies.

2 cups masa harina (see Helpful
    Hints, page 57)
2 cups low-fat milk or soy milk
½ teaspoon turmeric
2 teaspoons canola oil
1 medium yellow onion, diced
1 green bell pepper, seeded
    and diced
2 ribs celery, diced
One 15-ounce can crushed
    tomatoes
One 15-ounce can black beans,
    drained
1 tablespoon commercial taco
    seasoning (see Helpful
    Hint, page 19)
⅓ cup shredded low-fat Swiss
    or cheddar cheese

Preheat the oven to 400°F.

In a mixing bowl, combine the masa harina, milk, and turmeric and blend into a moist dough. Spread the dough onto two lightly greased 9-inch pie pans. With the back of a spoon, spread the dough evenly over the bottoms and up the sides of the pans. Place the pans in the oven and bake until the crust is dry, 12 to 14 minutes. Remove from the heat.

Meanwhile, in a large saucepan, heat the oil over medium heat. Add the onion, bell pepper, and celery and cook, stirring, until the onion is translucent, about 6 minutes. Stir in the crushed tomatoes, beans, and taco seasoning and bring to a simmer. Cook for 10 minutes over medium-low heat, stirring occasionally.

When the crusts are ready, ladle the bean mixture over the top of each crust. Sprinkle with cheese and place in the oven. Bake until the cheese is melted, about 5 minutes. Remove from the heat and cut each pie into 4 wedges. Use a wide spatula to transfer the pie to serving plates.

Makes 6 to 8 servings

Per serving:
274 Calories; 12g Protein; 5g Fat; 51g Carbohydrates; 9mg Cholesterol; 452mg Sodium; 7g Fiber

Skillet Vegetable and Tofu Burritos

1¼ cups white rice
2½ cups water
2 teaspoons canola oil
1 green bell pepper, seeded
    and diced
1 medium zucchini, diced
One 14-ounce can artichoke
    hearts, drained
One 14-ounce can corn kernels,
    drained
4 ounces extra-firm tofu, diced
2 teaspoons dried oregano
½ teaspoon salt
½ teaspoon freshly ground
    black pepper
Four 10-inch flour tortillas
1 cup tomato salsa

In a medium saucepan, combine the rice and water and bring to a simmer over medium-high heat. Stir the rice, cover, reduce heat to medium-low and cook until tender, 12 to 15 minutes. Fluff the grains with a fork and let stand, covered, for 5 minutes.

Meanwhile, in a medium saucepan, heat the oil over medium-high heat. Add the bell pepper and zucchini and cook, stirring, until tender, about 6 minutes. Stir in the artichokes, corn, tofu, oregano, salt, and pepper and cook over medium heat, stirring, until warmed through, about 4 minutes.

Warm the tortillas over a hot burner or pan and place on large serving plates. Spoon the rice down the center of each tortilla and top with the vegetable mixture and salsa. Roll the tortillas around the filling, creating burritos, and serve at once.

**Makes 4 burritos
(4 servings)**

Per serving:
484 Calories; 17g Protein; 6g Fat;
93g Carbohydrates; 6mg Cholesterol; 1,791mg Sodium; 15g Fiber

Corn and White Bean Ratatouille

Here is a Mexican-inspired twist on a Mediterranean standard.

1½ tablespoons canola oil

1 medium yellow onion, diced

1 medium zucchini, diced

2 cups diced eggplant

4 cloves garlic, minced

One 28-ounce can plum tomatoes, undrained

One 15-ounce can white kidney beans, drained

One 11-ounce can corn kernels, drained

1 tablespoon chopped pickled jalapeños (optional)

1 tablespoon dried parsley

2 teaspoons dried oregano

¼ teaspoon cayenne pepper

½ teaspoon salt

In a large saucepan, heat the oil over medium heat. Add the onion, zucchini, eggplant, and garlic and cook, stirring, until tender, 8 to 10 minutes. Stir in the remaining ingredients, reduce heat, and cook for 15 minutes, stirring occasionally. While cooking, cut the plum tomatoes into smaller pieces with a spoon.

Remove the ratatouille from the heat and let stand for 5 minutes. Serve with rice or pasta.

Makes 4 servings

Per serving:
249 Calories; 10g Protein; 6g Fat; 42g Carbohydrates; 0 Cholesterol; 1,280mg Sodium; 9g Fiber

Breakfast Burrito with Red Beans and Rice

Here is a flavorful way to transform leftover rice into a savory morning dish. The burrito is a healthy alternative to omelets or butter-drenched pancakes.

2 teaspoons canola oil
1 green bell pepper, seeded
and diced
1 medium zucchini, diced
2 cups cooked white or brown
rice (see Helpful Hint)
One 15-ounce can red kidney
beans or pinto beans,
drained
4 whole scallions, trimmed
and chopped
¼ cup chopped fresh parsley
½ teaspoon ground cumin
½ teaspoon salt
½ teaspoon freshly ground
black pepper
1 large egg plus 1 large egg
white, beaten
Four 10-inch flour tortillas
1 cup salsa or taco sauce

In a large nonstick skillet, heat the oil over medium heat. Add the pepper and zucchini and cook, stirring, until tender, about 5 minutes. Stir in the rice, beans, scallions, parsley, cumin, salt, and pepper and cook, stirring, until the mixture is steaming, about 4 minutes. Blend in the eggs and cook, stirring, until the eggs are completely cooked, about 4 minutes.

Warm the flour tortillas over a hot burner or skillet and place on large serving plates. Spoon the rice mixture down the center of the tortillas. Roll the tortillas around the filling, creating burritos. Spoon the salsa over the tops.

Makes 4 burritos
(4 servings)

Helpful Hint

For 2 cups of cooked rice, combine about ¾ cup uncooked rice with 1½ cups water and cook, covered, until tender.

Per serving:
422 Calories; 16g Protein; 7g Fat; 76g Carbohydrates; 53mg Cholesterol; 1,508mg Sodium; 12g Fiber

Lentils with Gourmet Squash

Young zucchini and pattypan squash give this hearty lentil stew a savory twist. To speed up the cooking time, presoak the lentils.

1 tablespoon canola oil
1 medium yellow onion, diced
1 rib celery, chopped
4 cloves garlic, minced
7 cups water
1 cup green lentils, rinsed or soaked
2 cups peeled and diced butternut squash
1 teaspoon ground cumin
1 teaspoon ground coriander
½ teaspoon freshly ground black pepper
10 to 12 whole baby pattypan squash or baby zucchini
¼ cup chopped fresh parsley
1 teaspoon salt

In a large saucepan, heat the oil over medium heat. Add the onion, celery, and garlic and cook, stirring, until tender, about 5 minutes. Stir in the water and lentils and bring to a simmer. Cook for 10 minutes over medium heat, stirring occasionally. Stir in the butternut squash, cumin, coriander, and pepper and cook for 10 minutes. Stir in the baby squash and cook until the lentils are tender, about 10 minutes. Stir in the parsley and salt, and let stand for 5 to 10 minutes before serving.

Ladle the stew into bowls and serve with warm flour tortillas.

Makes 6 servings

Per serving:
180 Calories; 10g Protein; 3g Fat; 31g Carbohydrates; 0 Cholesterol; 401mg Sodium; 10g Fiber

Chayote Pancakes

*Shredded chayote adds a light vegetable nuance
to these tasty potato pancakes.*

**1 medium chayote, seeded and
   shredded (about 2 cups),
   (see Helpful Hints, page 57)**
**1 white potato, peeled and
   shredded (about 2 cups)**
1 small yellow onion, shredded
1 large egg, beaten
¼ cup bread crumbs
½ teaspoon salt
**½ teaspoon freshly ground
   black pepper**
2 teaspoons canola oil
**1 cup tomato salsa or salsa
   verde (optional)**

Place the chayote, potato, and onion in a colander and squeeze out the excess moisture. Transfer to a mixing bowl and blend in the egg, bread crumbs, and seasonings.

In a large skillet, heat the oil over medium heat. Scoop about ½ cup of the batter and drop into the skillet forming a 3- to 4-inch pancake. Cook, flipping once, until both sides are lightly browned, about 4 minutes per side. Place on a warm plate and cover. Continue the process with the remaining batter.

If desired, serve the pancakes with tomato salsa or salsa verde.

**Makes 5 pancakes
(5 servings)**

Per serving:
95 Calories; 3g Protein; 3g Fat;
14g Carbohydrates; 42mg Cholesterol; 295mg Sodium; 2g Fiber

Artichoke-Rice Burrito with White Beans

*The combination of artichokes, rice, and white beans
makes for a hearty and delectable filling.*

2 tablespoons canola oil
2 medium yellow onions, diced
2 large cloves garlic, minced
2 cups water
1 cup long-grain white rice
**One 14-ounce can artichokes,
  rinsed and coarsely
  chopped**
2 teaspoons dried oregano
½ teaspoon turmeric
½ teaspoon salt
**½ teaspoon freshly ground
  black pepper**
1 cup frozen green peas
**Two 15-ounce cans white
  kidney beans**
¼ cup chopped fresh parsley
Four 10-inch flour tortillas
½ cup low-fat plain yogurt
**Salsa or taco sauce to taste
  (optional)**

In a medium saucepan, heat
1 tablespoon oil over medium
heat. Add 1 diced onion and the
garlic and cook, stirring, until
tender, 4 minutes. Stir in the
water, rice, artichokes, oregano,
turmeric, salt, and pepper and
bring to a simmer. Stir in the peas,
cover, reduce heat to medium-low,
and cook until all of the liquid is
absorbed, about 15 minutes. Fluff
the rice and let stand, covered, for
5 minutes.

Meanwhile, drain the beans
and reserve ¼ cup liquid.

In another saucepan, heat the
remaining 1 tablespoon oil over
medium heat. Add the remaining
onion and cook, stirring, until
tender, about 4 minutes. Stir in
the beans, bean liquid, and
parsley and bring to a simmer.
Cook over medium-low heat,
stirring, until heated through,
about 5 minutes. Transfer to a
blender or a food processor fitted
with a steel blade and process
until smooth, about 5 seconds.
Return the beans to the saucepan
and keep warm.

When the rice is done, warm
the flour tortillas over a hot
burner or skillet and place on
large serving plates. Spoon the
rice mixture and then the bean
puree down the center of the
tortillas. Spoon about 2 tablespoons of yogurt over the top of
each filling. Roll the tortillas
around the filling, creating
burritos. If desired, serve with
salsa or taco sauce.

Makes 4 servings

Per serving:
632 Calories, 24g Protein; 11g Fat;
110g Carbohydrates; 1mg Cholesterol; 1,439mg Sodium; 16 Fiber

Eggplant, Corn, and Tofu Stew

This is a hearty posole-style stew brimming with flavors and sustenance.

1 tablespoon canola oil
1 medium yellow onion, diced
1 green bell pepper, seeded
    and diced
2 cups diced eggplant
3 to 4 cloves garlic, minced
One 28-ounce can plum toma-
    toes, undrained
One 11-ounce can corn kernels,
    drained
4 ounces extra-firm tofu, diced
2 teaspoons dried oregano
1 teaspoon chili powder
½ teaspoon salt
½ teaspoon freshly ground
    black pepper

In a large saucepan, heat the oil over medium heat. Add the onion, bell pepper, eggplant, and garlic and cook, stirring, until tender, about 8 minutes. Stir in the remaining ingredients and bring to a simmer. Cook for 15 to 20 minutes over medium-low heat, stirring occasionally. (Cut the tomatoes into smaller pieces with a spoon.)

Let stand for 5 to 10 minutes before serving. Ladle the stew into bowls and serve with warm tortillas or corn bread. Rice makes a natural accompaniment.

Makes 4 servings

Per serving:
187 Calories; 8g Protein; 6g Fat;
27g Carbohydrates; 0 Cholesterol;
919mg Sodium; 5g Fiber

Quesadilla Grande

For this simple, plate-sized quesadilla, two humble staples, rice and beans, are topped with salsa and yogurt and transformed into a dish worthy of gourmet status.

1¼ cups white rice
2½ cups water
Two 15-ounce cans pinto beans
2 teaspoons canola oil
1 medium yellow onion, diced
4 whole scallions, trimmed and chopped
1½ tablespoons commercial taco seasoning (see Helpful Hint, page 19)
Four 12-inch flour tortillas
1 cup tomato salsa
½ cup low-fat plain yogurt

In a medium saucepan, combine the rice and water and bring to a simmer over medium-high heat. Stir the rice, reduce heat to medium-low, cover, and cook until tender, 12 to 15 minutes. Fluff the grains and let stand, covered, for 5 minutes.

Drain the beans, reserving ½ cup of the liquid. In a medium saucepan, heat the oil over medium heat. Add the onion and cook, stirring, until tender, about 4 minutes. Add the beans, reserved liquid, scallions, taco seasoning, and cook, stirring, 7 to 8 minutes.

Warm the flour tortillas over a hot burner or in a skillet and place on large serving plates. Spoon the rice over one-half of each tortilla. Top with the beans, salsa, and yogurt. Fold the remaining half of the tortilla over each filling and press down slightly. Serve the quesadillas immediately.

Makes 4 large quesadillas (6 servings)

Helpful Hint

If 12-inch "supersize" flour tortillas are not available, 10-inch flour tortillas can be used.

Per serving:
365 Calories; 13g Protein; 3g Fat; 72g Carbohydrates; 1mg Cholesterol; 1,372mg Sodium; 13g Fiber

Sopa Seca de Fideos
BAKED PASTA CASSEROLE

Sopa seca, *which means "dry soup," refers to dishes cooked in a robust, highly flavored brothy sauce. This* sopa seca *is made with thin vermicelli noodles.*

12 ounces thin spaghetti or vermicelli

2 teaspoons canola oil

1 medium yellow onion, diced

1 green bell pepper, seeded and diced

2 cloves garlic, minced

One 28-ounce can tomato puree

One 15-ounce can red kidney beans, drained

½ cup water

2 teaspoons dried oregano

1 teaspoon dried basil

½ teaspoon freshly ground black pepper

½ cup shredded low-fat Monterey Jack cheese

In a medium saucepan, bring 3 quarts of water to a boil over medium-high heat. Place the noodles in the boiling water, stir, and return to a boil. Cook until *al dente,* 6 to 8 minutes, stirring occasionally. Drain in a colander.

Preheat the oven to 400°F.

In a medium saucepan, heat the oil over medium heat. Add the onion, bell pepper, and garlic and cook, stirring, until the vegetables are tender, about 5 minutes. Add the tomato puree, beans, water, and seasonings and bring to a simmer. Cook for 10 minutes over medium heat, stirring occasionally.

Ladle about half of the sauce into a 9×13-inch casserole dish and spread evenly over the bottom. Spread the noodles evenly on top, and cover with another layer of sauce. Sprinkle the cheese over the top. Bake until the cheese is melted, about 5 minutes. Serve with warm bread.

Makes 6 servings

Per serving:
151 Calories; 5g Protein; 3g Fat; 28g Carbohydrates; 0 Cholesterol; 424mg Sodium; 3g Fiber

Portobello Burritos with Spinach and Goat Cheese

Woodsy, firm-textured portobello mushrooms make an appealing filling for burritos. The mushrooms are complemented by thyme, garlic, and goat cheese.

1 tablespoon canola oil
1 tablespoon dry white wine
2 medium portobello mushrooms, diced
1 medium yellow onion, diced
1 red bell pepper, seeded and diced
4 cloves garlic, minced
6 cups shredded fresh spinach
8 ounces extra-firm tofu, diced
½ teaspoon dried thyme
½ teaspoon salt
½ teaspoon freshly ground black pepper
Four 10-inch flour tortillas
¼ cup chèvre (smooth goat cheese)
1 cup tomato salsa (optional)

In a large saucepan, heat the oil and wine over medium heat. Add the mushrooms, onion, bell pepper, and garlic and cook, stirring, until tender, about 7 minutes. Stir in the spinach, tofu, thyme, salt, and pepper and cook, stirring, until the spinach is wilted, about 4 minutes.

Warm the flour tortillas over a hot burner or skillet and place on large serving plates. Spread about 1 tablespoon of chèvre over each tortilla. Spoon the mushroom mixture down the center of the tortillas. Roll the tortillas around the filling, creating burritos. If desired, spoon the salsa over the top of the burritos.

VARIATIONS

Part-skim ricotta can be substituted for the goat cheese.

Rice makes a natural side dish.

Makes 4 burritos (4 servings)

Per serving:
308 Calories; 16g Protein; 11g Fat; 39g Carbohydrates; 3mg Cholesterol; 569mg Sodium; 5g Fiber

Stuffed Poblano Chili Peppers

The sturdy flesh and mild heat of poblano chilies make them an ideal candidate for stuffed or baked dishes.

3 cups cooked white rice or brown rice (see Helpful Hint, page 36)
½ teaspoon salt
½ teaspoon freshly ground black pepper
4 large poblano chilies
One 16-ounce can vegetarian refried beans
½ cup tomato salsa
½ cup low-fat plain yogurt

Preheat the oven to 375°F.

In a medium mixing bowl, combine the rice, salt, and pepper. Set aside.

Slit the poblano chilies in half lengthwise and remove the seeds. (Wear rubber gloves to protect your skin.) Fill each pod with the rice mixture. Arrange the stuffed poblanos in a casserole dish or baking pan and place in the oven. Bake until the poblanos are tender and the outer skin is bubbly, 15 to 20 minutes. Remove from the oven and set aside.

Meanwhile, add the refried beans to a medium saucepan over medium heat and bring to a gentle simmer. Cook over medium-low heat, stirring, until the beans are steaming, about 5 minutes.

Place the stuffed poblanos on serving plates and spoon the beans over the top or on the side. Top each poblano with the salsa and yogurt. Serve at once.

Makes 4 servings

VARIATIONS

Large green or red bell peppers can be used if poblanos are unavailable.

Per serving:
294 Calories; 11g Protein; 1g Fat; 61g Carbohydrates; 2mg Cholesterol; 981mg Sodium; 5g Fiber

Tomato, Rice, and Tofu Burrito

*Smooth-textured tofu gives the illusion of cheese in this burrito.
A green sauce such as salsa verde or guacamole will
complement the tomato-based rice filling.*

2 cups water
1 cup white long-grain rice
½ teaspoon turmeric
1 tablespoon canola oil
1 medium yellow onion, diced
**8 ounces fresh white mush-
     rooms, sliced**
2 cloves garlic, minced
8 ounces extra-firm tofu, diced
**One 14-ounce can stewed
     tomatoes, undrained**
2 teaspoons dried oregano
½ teaspoon salt
**½ teaspoon freshly ground
     black pepper**
Four 10-inch flour tortillas
½ cup salsa verde or guacamole

In a medium saucepan, combine
the water, rice, and turmeric.
Bring to a simmer; reduce heat to
medium-low, then stir the rice,
cover the pan, and cook until all
of the liquid is absorbed, about
15 minutes. Fluff the grains with
a fork and let stand, covered, for
5 minutes.

Meanwhile, in a medium
saucepan, heat the oil over
medium heat. Add the onion,
mushrooms, and garlic and cook,
stirring, until tender, about
6 minutes. Stir in the tofu and
cook, stirring, for another
2 minutes. Add the stewed
tomatoes and liquid, oregano,
salt, and pepper and bring to a
simmer. Cook for 5 minutes,
stirring occasionally. Fold in the
cooked rice.

Warm the tortillas over a hot
burner or in a skillet and place on
large serving plates. Spoon the
rice mixture down the center of
each tortilla. Roll the tortillas
around the filling, creating
burritos. Spoon the salsa verde
on the side and serve at once.

**Makes 4 burritos
(4 servings)**

Per serving:
413 Calories; 17g Protein; 8g Fat;
70g Carbohydrates; 0 Cholesterol;
1,100mg Sodium; 14g Fiber

Rice-Filled Quesadillas with Avocado Salsa

An easy way to jazz up a commercial salsa is to mix in a ripe avocado.

1½ cups white rice
3 cups water
Two 15-ounce cans black beans, undrained
2 teaspoons canola oil
1 medium yellow onion, diced
1 tablespoon commercial taco seasoning (see Helpful Hint, page 19)
1 large ripe avocado, peeled, pitted, and diced (see Helpful Hints, page 11)
1½ cups tomato salsa
Six 7-inch flour tortillas

In a medium saucepan, combine the rice and water and bring to a simmer over medium-high heat. Stir the rice, cover, and cook over medium-low heat until tender, 12 to 15 minutes. Fluff the grains with a fork and let stand, covered, for 5 minutes.

Drain the beans, reserving ½ cup of the liquid. In a medium saucepan, heat the oil over medium heat. Add the onion and cook, stirring, until tender, about 4 minutes. Add the beans, reserved liquid, taco seasoning and cook, stirring, 7 to 8 minutes.

In a small mixing bowl, combine the avocado and salsa. Set aside.

Warm the flour tortillas over a hot burner or skillet and place on serving plates. Spoon the rice over one-half of each tortilla. Top with the beans and avocado-salsa mixture. Fold the remaining half of the tortillas over each filling and press down slightly. Serve the quesadillas immediately.

**Makes 6 small quesadillas
(6 servings)**

Per serving:
359 Calories; 12g Protein; 7g Fat; 67g Carbohydrates; 0 Cholesterol; 1,500mg Sodium; 16g Fiber

Tacqueria Tacos

*These "rush hour" tacos are easy to make and are
filled with the works. Feel free to improvise.*

**One 16-ounce can vegetarian
   refried beans**
6 taco shells
**8 leaves romaine lettuce,
   shredded**
**1 ripe avocado, peeled, pitted,
   and sliced (see Helpful
   Hints, page 11)**
2 tomatoes, diced
1 medium red onion, chopped
½ cup taco sauce
**6 tablespoons shredded low-fat
   Monterey Jack cheese
   (optional)**

Preheat the oven to 350°F.

Add the refried beans to a
medium saucepan. Cook, stirring,
over medium heat until the beans
are steaming, 4 to 5 minutes.

Meanwhile, arrange the taco
shells on a large baking pan. Place
in the oven and bake for 5 to 6
minutes. Remove from the oven
and place on a serving platter.

Fill each taco with 3 to 4
tablespoons of the beans. Top with
the lettuce, avocado slices, tomatoes, onion, taco sauce, and cheese
if desired. Serve the tacos at once.

Makes 6 tacos (6 servings)

VARIATIONS

*Other taco fillings include pickled
jalapeños, guacamole,* chili
rajas, *succotash, salsa verde,
or cooked rice.*

Per serving:
236 Calories; 8g Protein; 7g Fat; 35g
Carbohydrates; 5mg Cholesterol;
561mg Sodium; 7g Fiber

Burrito Pilaf with Winter Squash

Butternut squash, rice, and mushrooms form an enticing filling for these hearty burritos. No one will leave the table feeling hungry after this meal.

2 tablespoons canola oil
2 medium yellow onions, chopped
8 ounces fresh white mushrooms, sliced
1 large rib celery, chopped
2 cloves garlic, minced (optional)
2 cups water
2 cups peeled and diced butternut squash
1 cup white rice
½ teaspoon turmeric
½ teaspoon salt
½ teaspoon freshly ground black pepper
Two 15-ounce cans red kidney beans, undrained
1 teaspoon ground cumin
Four 10-inch flour tortillas
½ cup low-fat plain yogurt

In a large saucepan, heat 1 tablespoon oil over medium heat. Add 1 chopped onion, mushrooms, celery, and garlic if desired and cook, stirring, until tender, about 6 minutes. Add the water, squash, rice, turmeric, salt, and pepper and bring to a simmer. Cover, reduce heat to medium-low, and cook until all of the liquid is absorbed, 15 to 20 minutes. Fluff the rice with a fork and let stand, covered, for 5 minutes.

Meanwhile, drain the beans and reserve ¼ cup of the liquid. In a medium saucepan, heat the remaining 1 tablespoon oil over medium heat. Add the remaining onion and cook, stirring, until tender, about 4 minutes. Add the beans, bean liquid, and cumin and cook, stirring, until beans are heated through, 5 to 7 minutes. Transfer the beans to a blender and process until smooth, about 5 seconds, stopping to stir at least once. Return the beans to the pan and keep warm over low heat.

When the pilaf is done, warm the flour tortillas over a hot burner or skillet and place on large serving plates. Spoon the pilaf down the center of the tortillas; follow with the pureed beans. Spoon about 2 tablespoons of yogurt over the top of each filling. Roll the tortillas around the filling, creating burritos, and serve at once.

Makes 4 burritos
(4 servings)

Per serving:
620 Calories, 21g Protein; 11g Fat; 112g Carbohydrates; 2mg Cholesterol; 1,157mg Sodium; 16g Fiber

Ranchero Stew with Tempeh and Tomatoes

For this rustic, country-style stew, tempeh replaces the meat and joins tomatoes, vegetables, and assertive spices.

1 tablespoon canola oil
1 medium yellow onion, diced
1 green bell pepper, seeded
    and diced
2 ribs celery, diced
3 to 4 cloves garlic, minced
One 28-ounce can crushed
    tomatoes
One 14-ounce can stewed
    tomatoes, undrained
8 ounces tempeh, diced
1 tablespoon chili powder
1 tablespoon dried oregano
1½ teaspoons ground cumin
½ teaspoon salt
½ teaspoon freshly ground
    black pepper

In a large saucepan, heat the oil over medium heat. Add the onion, bell pepper, celery, and garlic and cook, stirring, until tender, about 5 minutes. Stir in the remaining ingredients and bring to a simmer. Reduce heat to medium-low and cook for 15 minutes, stirring occasionally.

Ladle the stew into bowls and serve at once. Serve rice, pasta, or couscous as a side dish.

Makes 6 servings

VARIATIONS

Serve the stew with a topping such as shredded low-fat cheese, scallions, or chopped red onions.

Per serving:
184 Calories; 11g Protein; 8g Fat;
20g Carbohydrates; 0 Cholesterol;
1,054mg Sodium; 7g Fiber

Yucatán Pasta with Habanero Tomato Sauce

This pasta dish is electrified with the extremely hot habanero pepper. Note that the habanero is left whole, so you can remove it before serving. If you are brave, you can mince the chili and leave it in; be sure to wear gloves if you chop it to avoid burning your fingers.

1 tablespoon canola oil
1 medium yellow onion, diced
2 large cloves garlic, minced
One 28-ounce can plum
    tomatoes, undrained
¼ cup chopped fresh parsley
1 fresh habanero pepper,
    pierced with a fork
    several times
2 teaspoons dried oregano
1 teaspoon ground cumin
½ teaspoon salt
½ teaspoon freshly ground
    black pepper
1 to 3 teaspoons habanero
    hot sauce, or to taste
12 ounces spaghetti
Grated Parmesan cheese
    (optional)

In a large saucepan, heat the oil over medium heat. Add the onion and garlic and cook, stirring, until tender, about 4 minutes. Add the tomatoes, parsley, habanero, oregano, cumin, salt, and pepper and bring to a simmer. Reduce heat to medium-low and cook, stirring occasionally, 15 to 20 minutes.

Remove the habanero from the sauce and discard. Transfer the sauce to a blender or food processor fitted with a steel blade and process until smooth, about 5 seconds. Return the sauce to the pan and add the bottled habanero sauce to taste. Keep warm until the pasta is ready.

In a large saucepan, bring 3 quarts of water to a boil over medium-high heat. Place the noodles in the boiling water, stir, and return to a boil. Cook until *al dente,* about 10 minutes, stirring occasionally. Drain the pasta in a colander. Transfer the noodles to warm serving dishes and ladle the sauce over the top. If desired, served with grated Parmesan cheese.

Makes 4 servings

Per serving:
331 Calories; 10g Protein; 5g Fat; 60g Carbohydrates; 0 Cholesterol; 948mg Sodium; 6g Fiber

VARIATION

If habanero pepper sauce is not available, try a traditional Louisiana hot sauce. The sauce will be less hot, but still flavorful.

Avocado, Bean, and Corn Burrito

These light-hearted, cheeseless tortillas can be ready in a jiffy. Avocado adds a luscious texture while lime provides a refreshing flavor.

One 15-ounce can corn kernels, drained
One 15-ounce can red kidney beans or black beans, drained
2 ribs celery, diced
1 tomato, diced
1 ripe avocado, peeled, pitted, and diced (see Helpful Hints, page 11)
4 whole scallions, trimmed and chopped
2 cloves garlic, minced
Juice of 1 large lime
2 teaspoons dried oregano
1 teaspoon ground cumin
½ teaspoon salt
½ teaspoon freshly ground black pepper
Four 10-inch flour tortillas
1 cup tomato salsa

Combine all of the ingredients, except the tortillas and salsa, in a medium saucepan and blend thoroughly. Cook over medium heat, stirring frequently, until the mixture is steaming, about 5 minutes.

Warm the tortillas over a hot burner or in a skillet and place on large serving plates. Spoon the avocado-vegetable mixture down the center of each tortilla. Roll the tortillas around the filling, creating burritos. Spoon the salsa over the top of the burritos and serve at once.

**Makes 4 burritos
(4 servings)**

Per serving:
412 Calories; 13g Protein; 10g Fat;
72g Carbohydrates; 0 Cholesterol;
1,697mg Sodium; 17g Fiber

Bell Pepper Rellenos

Rellenos means "stuffed," and these peppers can be stuffed with just about any leftover pilaf or rice dish. For best results, choose block-shaped peppers that will stand upright in a baking pan.

3 cups cooked white rice, brown rice (see Helpful Hint, page 36), or leftover pilaf

2 large whole scallions, trimmed and chopped

½ teaspoon salt

½ teaspoon freshly ground black pepper

6 large red or green bell peppers, tops sliced off, cored and seeded

1 cup tomato salsa or taco sauce

Two 15-ounce cans red kidney beans or pinto beans, undrained

2 tablespoons commercial taco seasoning (see Helpful Hint, page 19)

¾ cup low-fat plain yogurt

Preheat the oven to 400°F.

In a medium mixing bowl, combine the cooked rice, scallions, salt, and black pepper.

Fill each pepper with the rice mixture. Place the peppers in an upright position in a casserole dish or baking pan and spoon 1 to 2 tablespoons of salsa over the top of each. Place in the oven and bake until the peppers are tender, about 20 minutes. Remove from the oven and keep warm until the beans are done.

Meanwhile, drain the beans and reserve ½ cup of the liquid. Add the beans, bean liquid, and taco seasoning to a medium saucepan and bring to a gentle simmer over medium heat. Cook over medium-low heat, stirring, until the beans are steaming, about 5 minutes. To thicken, mash the beans against the side of the pan with the back of a large spoon.

Place the stuffed peppers in the center of round serving plates and spoon the beans around each pepper. Top the peppers with yogurt and serve at once.

Makes 6 servings

Per serving:
222 Calories; 9g Protein; 1g Fat; 44g Carbohydrates; 2mg Cholesterol; 913mg Sodium; 8g Fiber

Corn and White Bean Chili

For a hearty main entrée, serve this colorful cauldron over rice or pasta.

1 tablespoon canola oil
1 medium yellow onion, diced
1 red bell pepper, seeded and
**   diced**
1 medium zucchini, diced
1 large carrot, peeled and diced
2 large cloves garlic, minced
One 28-ounce can plum
**   tomatoes, undrained**
One 15-ounce can corn kernels,
**   drained**
One 15-ounce can white kidney
**   beans, drained**
1 tablespoon dried parsley
1 tablespoon dried oregano
1 tablespoon chili powder
½ teaspoon salt
½ teaspoon freshly ground
**   black pepper**

In a large saucepan, heat the oil over medium heat. Add the onion, bell pepper, zucchini, carrot, and garlic and cook, stirring, until tender, about 7 minutes. Stir in the remaining ingredients and bring to a simmer. Cook for 15 to 20 minutes over medium-low heat, stirring occasionally.

Remove the chili from the heat and let stand for 5 minutes before serving. Ladle into bowls and serve with cornbread or warm flour tortillas.

Makes 6 servings

Per serving:
159 Calories; 7g Protein; 3g Fat;
27g Carbohydrates; 0 Cholesterol;
837mg Sodium; 7g Fiber

Morning Rice and Beans

Who says rice and beans should be limited to lunch or dinner? Making them for breakfast is a great way to use up leftover rice and vegetables.

1 tablespoon canola oil
1 small yellow onion, chopped
1 red bell pepper, seeded and
    diced
1 to 2 cloves garlic, minced
4 cups cooked brown or
    white rice (see Helpful
    Hints, page 57)
One 15-ounce can black beans,
    drained
3 to 4 tablespoons chopped
    fresh parsley
1 tablespoon chopped pickled
    jalapeños (optional)
2 to 3 teaspoons vegetarian
    Worcestershire sauce
    (see Helpful Hint)
1 teaspoon dried oregano
½ teaspoon ground cumin
½ teaspoon salt
½ teaspoon freshly ground
    black pepper

In a large nonstick skillet, heat the oil over medium heat. Add the onion, bell pepper, and garlic and cook, stirring, until tender, about 5 minutes. Add the remaining ingredients and cook, stirring, about 10 minutes.

Spoon the mixture onto serving plates and serve with warm flour tortillas.

Makes 4 servings

Helpful Hint

There are several brands of Worcestershire sauce on the market that do not contain anchovies. Check the labels of the brands in your supermarket or natural food store to find a vegetarian version.

Per servings:
312 Calories; 9g Protein; 5g Fat;
61g Carbohydrates; 0 Cholesterol;
694mg Sodium; 9g Fiber

Sweet Potato and Rice Enchiladas

These enchiladas are no-fuss, well-stuffed tortillas that are snuggled together in a casserole dish and baked. Enchiladas can also be kept warm in the oven until everyone is ready to eat.

3 cups water
1½ cups long grain white rice or
    basmati rice
1 medium sweet potato, peeled
    and diced
¼ cup chopped fresh parsley
½ teaspoon salt
½ teaspoon freshly ground
    black pepper
One 15-ounce can black beans,
    drained
One 14-ounce can corn kernels,
    drained
3 to 4 whole scallions, trimmed
    and chopped
Six 10-inch flour tortillas
1½ cups enchilada sauce or
    taco sauce
½ cup shredded low-fat
    Monterey Jack cheese

Preheat the oven to 375°F.

In a medium saucepan, combine the water, rice, sweet potato, parsley, and seasonings and bring to a simmer over medium-high heat. Stir the rice, cover the pan, and cook over medium-low heat until all of the liquid is absorbed, about 15 minutes. Fluff the grains and potato with a fork and let stand, covered, for 5 minutes.

Meanwhile, in a medium mixing bowl, combine the black beans, corn, and scallions. Blend in the rice and potatoes. Place a tortilla on a flat surface and spoon about 1¼ cups of the mixture down the center. Wrap the tortilla around the filling and place in a lightly greased casserole dish or 9×13-inch baking pan. Continue filling the remaining tortillas and arrange side by side in the casserole dish. Drizzle the enchilada sauce over the top and sprinkle with shredded cheese. Place in the oven and bake until the cheese melts, about 5 minutes. Remove from the heat and serve at once.

**Makes 6 enchiladas
(6 servings)**

Per serving:
353 Calories; 13g Protein; 3g Fat; 23g Carbohydrates; 3mg Cholesterol; 883mg Sodium; 15g Fiber

Asian Burritos with Stir-Fried Vegetables

Like gourmet pizza, the burrito has become an international dish prepared with a variety of ethnic fillings. This Asian rendition includes bok choy, tofu, shiitake mushrooms, and soy sauce.

1 cup white rice
2 cups water
1 tablespoon canola oil
1 medium yellow onion, diced
1 green or red bell pepper,
seeded and diced
8 ounces fresh white
mushrooms, sliced
4 ounces fresh shiitake
mushrooms, sliced
2 teaspoons minced fresh
gingerroot (optional)
4 cups shredded bok choy
leaves
4 ounces extra-firm tofu, diced
2 to 3 tablespoons low-sodium
soy sauce
Four 10-inch flour tortillas
½ cup tomato salsa

In a medium saucepan, combine the rice and water and bring to a simmer over medium-high heat. Stir the rice, reduce the heat to medium-low, cook for 12 to 15 minutes. Fluff the grains with a fork and let stand, covered, for 5 minutes.

Meanwhile, in a large saucepan, heat the oil over medium-high. Add the onion, bell pepper, mushrooms, and ginger if desired and cook, stirring frequently, until tender, about 6 minutes. Stir in the bok choy and tofu and cook, stirring, until the greens are wilted, about 3 minutes. Fold in the cooked rice and soy sauce.

Warm the tortillas over a hot burner or in a skillet and place on large serving plates. Spoon the rice mixture down the center of each tortilla. Roll the tortillas around the filling, creating burritos. Serve the salsa on the side.

Makes 4 burritos
(4 servings)

Per serving:
412 Calories; 13g Protein; 8g Fat;
73g Carbohydrates; 0 Cholesterol;
1,040mg Sodium; 5g Fiber

Asparagus Quesadillas

An asparagus lover's quesadilla.

1 pound asparagus spears, trimmed and cut into 1-inch pieces
Four 10-inch flour tortillas
1 cup canned corn kernels, drained
½ cup jarred roasted red peppers, cut into strips
4 whole scallions, trimmed and chopped
2 tablespoons pickled jalapeño slices (optional)
½ to 1 cup tomato salsa
½ cup shredded low-fat Monterey Jack or Swiss cheese

Preheat the broiler.

In a medium saucepan, bring about 1 quart of water to a boil. Place the asparagus in the boiling water and cook over medium heat until tender, 3 to 4 minutes. Drain in a colander. (Alternatively, steam the asparagus until tender.)

Arrange the tortillas on two sheet pans. Fill the center of each flat tortilla with the corn, bell peppers, and asparagus, forming small mounds. Sprinkle the scallions and jalapeños if desired over the top. Follow with about 2 tablespoons of salsa and cheese. Place the tortillas beneath the broiler and broil until the cheese is melted, 2 to 3 minutes. Remove from the heat and fold the tortillas over the fillings, forming pockets. Using a wide spatula, transfer the quesadillas to serving plates and serve at once.

Makes 4 quesadillas
(4 servings)

Per serving:
239 Calories; 12g Protein; 4g Fat; 42g Carbohydrates; 10mg Cholesterol; 763mg Sodium; 15g Fiber

Black Bean and Avocado Burritos

Bigger than bite-size, but smaller than a dinner portion, these burritos also fit the bill as a substantial appetizer.

Two 15-ounce cans black beans, undrained
1 tablespoon canola oil
1 medium yellow onion, diced
2 large cloves garlic, minced
1 tablespoon chopped pickled jalapeños (optional)
2 teaspoons dried oregano
½ teaspoon salt
½ teaspoon freshly ground black pepper
Four 10-inch flour tortillas
2 ripe tomatoes, diced
1 ripe avocado, peeled, pitted, and sliced (see Helpful Hints, page 11)
4 whole scallions, trimmed and chopped

Drain the canned beans, reserving ½ cup of the liquid.

In a medium saucepan, heat the oil over medium-high heat. Add the onion and garlic and cook, stirring, until tender, about 4 minutes. Add the beans, bean liquid, jalapeños if desired, oregano, salt, and pepper. Reduce heat to medium-low and cook, stirring occasionally, until the beans are heated through, about 8 minutes. Transfer the beans to a blender or food processor fitted with a steel blade and process until smooth, about 5 seconds, stopping to stir at least once. Return the beans to the pan, reduce heat to low and cook, stirring, until heated through, about 5 minutes.

Meanwhile, warm the flour tortillas over a hot burner or skillet and place on serving plates. Spoon about ½ cup of the bean mixture down the center of each tortilla. Top the beans with the tomatoes, avocado slices, and scallions. Roll the tortillas around the filling, creating burritos, and serve at once.

Makes 4 burritos
(4 servings)

Per serving:
316 Calories, 11g Protein; 9g Fat; 55g Carbohydrates; 0 Cholesterol; 896mg Sodium; 12g Fiber

Nopales Gumbo
CACTUS GUMBO

*The okralike texture of nopales (fresh cactus paddles)
makes it a natural ingredient for a vegetable gumbo.*

1½ cups white rice
3 cups water
**2 medium fresh nopales (cactus
    paddles), about 5 ounces
    (see Helpful Hint, page 33)**
2 teaspoons canola oil
**1 medium yellow onion,
    chopped**
**1 green bell pepper, seeded
    and diced**
2 to 3 cloves garlic, minced
4 cups vegetable broth
**One 14-ounce can stewed
    tomatoes, undrained**
1 cup cooked red kidney beans
2 teaspoons dried oregano
½ teaspoon dried thyme
½ teaspoon salt
**½ teaspoon freshly ground
    black pepper**
¼ teaspoon cayenne pepper

In a medium saucepan, combine the rice and water and bring to a simmer over medium-high heat. Stir the rice, cover, and cook over medium-low heat until all of the liquid is absorbed, about 15 minutes. Fluff the grains with a fork and let stand, covered, for at least 5 minutes.

Meanwhile, prepare the nopales: Scrape off the prickly needles and bumps where the needles grew. (Careful, the needles are sharp.) Cut off the base and trim around the outer edge of the paddle. Cut the paddles in half across the width, then cut into ¼-inch-wide strips. The strips should resemble green beans.

In another medium saucepan, heat the oil over medium heat. Add the onion, bell pepper, and garlic and cook, stirring, until the vegetables are soft, about 5 minutes. Add the nopales and the remaining ingredients and bring to a simmer. Cook over medium heat until the nopales are tender, stirring occasionally, 12 to 15 minutes.

Spoon the rice into bowls and ladle the gumbo over the top. Serve at once.

Makes 6 servings

Per serving:
212 Calories; 7g Protein; 3g Fat;
41g Carbohydrates; 0 Cholesterol;
949mg Sodium; 5g Fiber

Pinto Bean and Soy Tacos

TVP (textured vegetable protein) replaces the ground meat in these finger-licking-good tacos. Plan to have plenty of napkins at the table.

2 teaspoons canola oil
1 small yellow onion, chopped
1 cup water or vegetable broth
1 cup TVP, mince-style
2 tablespoons commercial taco
   seasoning (see Helpful Hint,
   page 19)
One 15-ounce can pinto beans,
   drained
6 taco shells
6 to 8 leaves romaine lettuce,
   cut into strips
1 cup taco sauce
¾ cup low-fat plain yogurt

Preheat the oven to 350°F.

In a medium saucepan, heat the oil over medium heat. Add the onion and cook, stirring, until tender, about 4 minutes. Add the water, TVP, and taco seasoning and bring to a simmer. Cook over medium-low heat, stirring, until browned, about 5 minutes. Add the pinto beans and cook, stirring, until beans are heated through, about 5 minutes. Transfer the mixture to a warm serving bowl.

Meanwhile, arrange the taco shells on a large baking pan. Bake for 5 to 6 minutes. Remove from the oven and place on a serving platter.

Fill the tacos with 3 to 4 tablespoons of the bean mixture. Top each with the lettuce, 1 to 2 tablespoons taco sauce, and yogurt. Serve immediately.

**Makes 6 tacos
(6 servings)**

VARIATIONS

Other healthful taco fillings include chopped scallions or red onions, sprouts, or guacamole.

Per serving:
226 Calories; 17g Protein; 5g Fat; 31g Carbohydrates; 2mg Cholesterol; 868mg Sodium; 7g Fiber

Risotto Burrito with Sweet Potatoes

*The creamy nature of Arborio rice makes it a natural filling for a burrito.
Sweet potatoes and beans meld smoothly into the rice filling.*

1 tablespoon olive oil
1 medium yellow onion, diced
4 cloves garlic, minced
4 cups water
2 cups peeled and diced sweet
    potatoes
1 cup Arborio rice
½ teaspoon salt
½ teaspoon white pepper
One 15-ounce can red chili
    beans, drained
4 whole scallions, trimmed and
    chopped
⅓ cup freshly grated Parmesan
    cheese
Four 10-inch flour tortillas
1 cup tomato salsa or taco
    sauce

In a large saucepan, heat the oil over medium heat. Add the onion and garlic and cook, stirring, until tender, about 4 minutes. Add 2 cups water, sweet potatoes, rice, salt, and white pepper and bring to a simmer. Cook, uncovered, over medium heat, stirring frequently, about 10 minutes.

Stir in the remaining 2 cups water and cook, stirring, until the rice and potatoes are tender, about 15 minutes. Fold in the beans, scallions, and cheese.

Meanwhile, warm the flour tortillas over a hot burner or skillet and place on large serving plates. Spoon the risotto mixture down the center of the tortillas. Roll the tortillas around the filling, creating burritos. Serve the salsa on the side.

**Makes 4 burritos
(4 servings)**

Per serving:
590 Calories; 18g Protein; 9g Fat;
113g Carbohydrates; 6mg Cholesterol; 1,727mg Sodium; 13g Fiber

Mexican Primavera

Although rice is the favorite starch in Mexico, noodles (called fideo*) are also part of the national menu. This springtime dish of pasta and vegetables is enhanced with a touch of lemon and jalapeño peppers, Mexico's gift to the world.*

8 ounces vermicelli or thin spaghetti
2 teaspoons canola or olive oil
1 medium zucchini, halved lengthwise and thinly cut diagonally
1 green bell pepper, cut into slivers
2 cloves garlic, minced
1 jalapeño pepper, seeded and minced
2 tomatoes, diced
One 11-ounce can corn, drained
1 teaspoon dried oregano
½ teaspoon salt
Juice of 1 lemon
¼ cup freshly grated Parmesan cheese (optional)

VARIATIONS

Other seasonal vegetables, such as blanched asparagus, broccoli, green beans, or nopales (cactus paddles), can also be added to the pasta bowl.

In a large saucepan, bring 3 quarts of water to a boil over medium-high heat. Place the noodles in the boiling water, stir, and return to a boil. Cook until *al dente,* stirring occasionally, 5 to 8 minutes. Drain the noodles in a colander.

Meanwhile, in a large skillet, heat the oil over medium-high heat. Add the zucchini, bell pepper, garlic, and jalapeño and cook, stirring, until the vegetables are tender, about 6 minutes. Add the tomatoes, corn, oregano, and salt and cook, stirring until the mixture is steaming, about 4 minutes more.

In a large bowl, toss together the noodles, vegetables, lemon juice, and the cheese if desired. Serve at once.

Makes 4 servings

Per serving:
250 Calories; 8g Protein; 4g Fat;
50g Carbohydrates; 0 Cholesterol;
302mg Sodium; 5g Fiber

Couscous-Spinach Burrito with Feta and Black Olives

Couscous makes a light, fluffy filling for this Mediterranean-inspired burrito.

1 cup couscous
1½ cups boiling water
2 teaspoons canola oil
1 small yellow onion, finely
　chopped
2 cloves garlic, minced
6 cups fresh spinach leaves,
　coarsely chopped
Juice of 1 lemon
1 teaspoon dried oregano
½ teaspoon dried thyme
½ teaspoon salt
½ teaspoon freshly ground
　black pepper
½ cup jarred roasted red
　peppers, diced
⅓ cup sliced pitted black olives
Four 10-inch flour tortillas
2 ounces feta cheese, crumbled
Tomato salsa or taco sauce
　(optional)

In a medium bowl or saucepan, combine the couscous and boiling water. Cover and let stand for 10 minutes. Fluff the grains with a fork, cover, and set aside.

In a medium saucepan, heat the oil over medium heat. Add the onion and garlic and cook, stirring, until tender, about 3 minutes. Add the spinach, lemon juice, oregano, thyme, salt, and pepper and cook, stirring frequently, until the greens are wilted, about 4 minutes. Add the bell peppers and black olives and cook, stirring frequently, 2 to 3 minutes. Fold the couscous into the vegetables and blend thoroughly.

Meanwhile, warm the tortillas over a hot burner or in a skillet and place on large serving plates. Spoon the couscous-spinach mixture down the center of the tortillas. Sprinkle about 1 tablespoon of feta over the top of each filling. Roll the tortillas around the filling, creating burritos. If desired, serve with salsa or taco sauce.

**Makes 4 burritos
(4 servings)**

Per serving:
397 Calories; 15g Protein; 8g Fat; 68g Carbohydrates; 13mg Cholesterol; 967mg Sodium; 15g Fiber

Portobello and Tofu Fajitas

2 large cloves garlic, minced
3 tablespoons vegetarian
   Worcestershire sauce (see
   Helpful Hint, page 94)
1 tablespoon water
1½ tablespoons low-sodium
   soy sauce
Juice of 1 lime
2 tablespoons canola oil
2 teaspoons brown sugar
2 teaspoons dried oregano
4 to 5 portobello mushroom
   caps, thickly sliced
2 red bell peppers, cut into
   ½-inch-wide strips
1 large red onion, cut into
   ½-inch-wide strips
4 ounces extra-firm tofu, cut
   into matchstick strips
Four 10-inch flour tortillas
½ cup shredded low-fat
   Monterey Jack cheese
1 cup tomato salsa

Preheat the oven to 400°F.

In a medium mixing bowl, combine the garlic, Worcestershire sauce, water, soy sauce, lime juice, oil, brown sugar, and oregano. Set aside.

Place the mushrooms, peppers, onion, and tofu on a lightly sprayed large baking pan. Roast the vegetables until tender, 15 to 20 minutes. Add the roasted vegetables and tofu to the dressing and toss together thoroughly.

Warm the tortillas over a hot burner or skillet. With a slotted spoon, fill the tortillas with the vegetable mixture. Top with cheese and salsa, and serve at once.

Makes 4 fajitas
(4 servings)

VARIATION

The vegetables and tofu can also be grilled until they are tender over hot coals or a gas barbecue.

Per serving:
307 Calories; 13g Protein; 11g Fat; 42g Carbohydrates; 5mg Cholesterol; 1,080mg Sodium; 13g Fiber

Yellow Rice and Red Bean Burrito

Rice and beans are two quintessential fillings for a burrito. To speed things up, use jasmine rice, a grain that cooks in about 15 minutes.

1 cup white rice (preferably jasmine)
2 cups water
½ teaspoon turmeric
½ teaspoon salt
½ teaspoon freshly ground black pepper
1 tablespoon canola oil
1 medium yellow onion, diced
1 green or red bell pepper, seeded and diced
1 medium zucchini, diced
One 15-ounce can red kidney beans or black beans, drained
Four 10-inch flour tortillas
½ cup tomato salsa or guacamole

In a medium saucepan, combine the rice, water, turmeric, salt, and pepper. Bring to a simmer over medium-high heat. Stir the rice, reduce heat to medium-low, cover, and cook for 12 to 15 minutes. Fluff the grains with a fork and let stand, covered, for 5 minutes.

Meanwhile, in a medium saucepan, heat the oil over medium-high heat. Add the onion, bell pepper, and zucchini and cook, stirring, until tender, about 6 minutes. Stir in the beans and cook, stirring, until beans are heated, about 2 minutes. Fold in the cooked rice.

Warm the tortillas over a hot burner or in a skillet and place on large serving plates. Spoon the rice and bean mixture down the center of each tortilla. Roll the tortillas around the filling, creating burritos. Spoon the salsa over the top of the burritos and serve at once.

**Makes 4 burritos
(4 servings)**

Per serving:
454 Calories; 14g Protein; 7g Fat; 86g Carbohydrates; 0 Cholesterol; 1,136mg Sodium; 11g Fiber

Harvest Squash and Corn Stew

Squash, corn, and beans were favorite staples of the Mexican kitchen long before Columbus arrived in the New World.

1 tablespoon canola oil
1 medium yellow onion, diced
1 green bell pepper, seeded
    and diced
3 to 4 cloves garlic, minced
One 14-ounce can stewed
    tomatoes, undrained
2½ cups peeled and diced
    butternut squash or
    pumpkin
1 tablespoon dried oregano
1 tablespoon dried parsley
2 teaspoons paprika
½ teaspoon salt
½ teaspoon freshly ground
    black pepper
2 cups water or vegetable
    broth
One 11-ounce can corn kernels,
    drained
One 15-ounce can cranberry
    beans (see Helpful Hints) or
    red kidney beans, drained

In a large saucepan, heat the oil over medium heat. Add the onion, bell pepper, and garlic and cook, stirring, until tender, about 5 minutes. Add the tomatoes and liquid, squash, oregano, parsley, paprika, salt, and pepper and cook, stirring, for 3 to 4 minutes. Add the water, corn, and beans and bring to a simmer. Cook, stirring occasionally, over medium-low heat until the squash is tender, about 20 minutes.

Serve the stew over rice or quinoa.

Makes 6 servings

Helpful Hints

Cranberry beans, also called Roman beans, are available in most well-stocked supermarkets. Pink beans may be substituted.

Per serving:
176 Calories; 6g Protein; 3g Fat; 35g Carbohydrates; 0 Cholesterol; 689mg Sodium; 6g Fiber

Baked Tempeh Chilaquiles

Chilaquiles is the Mexican cousin of lasagna. The noodles are replaced with layers of corn tortillas. This version is filled with vegetables, tomatoes, and chewy tempeh.

2 teaspoons canola oil
1 medium yellow onion, diced
1 green bell pepper, seeded
    and diced
2 ribs celery, chopped
One 28-ounce can crushed
    tomatoes
¼ cup water
One 15-ounce can red kidney
    beans, drained
8 ounces tempeh, diced
2 tablespoons commercial taco
    seasoning (see Helpful Hint,
    page 19)
½ teaspoon salt
½ teaspoon freshly ground
    black pepper
Eight 6-inch corn tortillas,
    torn in half
¾ cup shredded low-fat
    Monterey Jack cheese
2 to 3 whole scallions, trimmed
    and chopped

Preheat the oven to 375°F.

In a large saucepan, heat the oil. Add the onion, bell pepper, and celery and cook, stirring, for 6 minutes. Stir in the crushed tomatoes, water, beans, tempeh, and seasonings and bring to a simmer. Cook over medium heat, stirring occasionally, about 10 minutes.

Cover the bottom of two 9-inch pie pans with a layer of tortilla halves (there will be some overlap). Place on each a layer about one-quarter of the tempeh mixture and 2 to 3 tablespoons cheese. Form another layer of tortilla halves, following again with the tempeh mixture and cheese. Sprinkle the scallions over the top and place the pans in the oven. Bake until the cheese is bubbly, about 10 minutes. Remove from the oven and let stand for 5 minutes before serving. Slice into pie-shaped wedges. Use a wide spatula to transfer the pie pieces to warm serving plates.

Makes 6 to 8 servings

Per serving:
247 Calories; 13g Protein; 5g Fat; 39g Carbohydrates; 10mg Cholesterol; 625mg Sodium; 9g Fiber

Tomatillo and Chickpea Ratatouille

Tomatillos add a Mexican undertone to this Mediterranean vegetable stew.

2 tablespoons dry red wine
1 tablespoon canola oil
1 medium yellow onion, diced
1 zucchini, diced
2 cups diced eggplant
12 fresh white mushrooms,
sliced
4 cloves garlic, minced
One 28-ounce can stewed or
diced tomatoes, undrained
6 medium tomatillos, diced
1 cup cooked chickpeas
1 tablespoon dried oregano
1 teaspoon dried basil
½ teaspoon salt
½ teaspoon freshly ground
black pepper

In a large saucepan, heat the wine and oil over medium heat. Add the onion, zucchini, eggplant, mushrooms, and garlic and cook, stirring, until tender, 8 to 10 minutes. Stir in the tomatoes and liquid, tomatillos, chickpeas, oregano, basil, salt, and pepper and bring to a simmer. Cook for 15 minutes, stirring occasionally. As the stew cooks, cut the tomatoes into smaller pieces with a spoon.

Remove the pan from the heat and let stand for about 5 minutes before serving. Serve the ratatouille over rice, quinoa, or pasta.

Makes 6 servings

Per serving:
155 Calories; 5g Protein; 3g Fat;
27g Carbohydrates; 0 Cholesterol;
599mg Sodium; 5g Fiber

Macaroni Magnifico

For this appealing version of sopa seca *(Mexican dry soup), macaroni is blended with tomatoes, artichoke hearts, tofu, and herbs.*

2 cups elbow macaroni
2 teaspoons canola oil
1 medium yellow onion, diced
1 green bell pepper, seeded
  and diced
One 28-ounce can plum
  tomatoes, undrained
One 14-ounce can artichoke
  hearts, rinsed and
  quartered
One 14-ounce can crushed
  tomatoes
8 ounces extra-firm tofu or
  tempeh, diced
2 teaspoons dried oregano
1 teaspoon dried basil
½ teaspoon salt
½ teaspoon freshly ground
  black pepper
½ cup shredded low-fat
  Monterey Jack cheese
  (optional)

In a medium saucepan, bring 2½ quarts of water to a boil over medium-high heat. Place the macaroni in the boiling water, stir, and cook until *al dente,* about 6 minutes, stirring occasionally. Drain in a colander.

Meanwhile, in a large saucepan, heat the oil over medium heat. Add the onion and bell pepper and cook, stirring, until the onion is translucent, about 5 minutes. Add the plum tomatoes and liquid, artichokes, crushed tomatoes, tofu, oregano, basil, salt, and pepper and bring to a simmer. Cook for 10 minutes over medium heat, stirring occasionally. As the mixture cooks, cut the tomatoes into small pieces with a spoon.

Fold the macaroni into the tomato mixture and cook for an additional 3 to 5 minutes over low heat. Ladle into large bowls and if desired, top with shredded cheese.

Makes 6 servings

Per serving:
243 Calories; 12g Protein; 4g Fat; 37g Carbohydrates; 0 Cholesterol; 471mg Sodium; 2g Fiber

Vegetable and Brown Rice Burritos

*Leftover brown rice finds new life in this bulging burrito
filled with vegetables and beans.*

1 tablespoon canola oil
8 to 10 fresh white mushrooms,
  sliced
1 green or red bell pepper,
  seeded and diced
2 cloves garlic, minced
2 cups cooked brown rice
  (see Helpful Hint, page 76)
One 15-ounce can red kidney
  beans or black beans,
  drained
1 cup corn kernels, fresh,
  frozen, or canned
2 large whole scallions,
  trimmed and chopped
½ teaspoon ground cumin
½ teaspoon freshly ground
  black pepper
Four 10-inch flour tortillas
½ cup shredded low-fat Swiss
  or Monterey Jack cheese
1 cup tomato salsa

In a large nonstick skillet, heat the oil over medium-high heat. Add the mushrooms, bell pepper, and garlic, and cook, stirring, until tender, 5 to 6 minutes. Stir in the rice, beans, corn, scallions, cumin, and pepper and cook over medium heat, stirring, for 4 to 6 minutes.

Warm the tortillas over a hot burner or in a skillet and place on large serving plates. Spoon the rice and bean mixture down the center of each tortilla. Top each with about 2 tablespoons of cheese and roll the tortillas around the filling, creating burritos. Spoon the salsa over the top of the burritos and serve at once.

**Makes 4 burritos
(4 servings)**

Per serving:
491 Calories; 19g Protein; 3g Fat;
83g Carbohydrates; 8mg Cholesterol; 1,351mg Sodium; 13g Fiber

Well-Filled Quesadillas with Sun-Dried Tomato Salsa

Sun-dried tomatoes create a salsa with a concentrated, rustic quality. The salsa is complemented with a filling of rice and beans.

1¼ cups white rice
2½ cups water
½ cup sun-dried tomatoes
  (not oil-packed)
1 large tomato, diced
¼ cup diced red onion
2 whole scallions, trimmed
  and chopped
2 tablespoons chopped cilantro
1 clove garlic, minced
1 tablespoon red wine vinegar
1 tablespoon canola oil
½ teaspoon salt
½ teaspoon freshly ground
  black pepper
Six 7-inch flour tortillas
One 16-ounce can refried beans,
  reheated
½ cup low-fat plain yogurt

In a medium saucepan, combine the rice and water and bring to a simmer over medium-high heat. Stir the rice, cover, and cook over medium-low heat, until tender, 12 to 15 minutes. Fluff the grains with a fork and let stand, covered, for 5 minutes.

In a small saucepan, bring 3 cups of water to a boil. Place the sun-dried tomatoes in the boiling water and cook over medium-low heat, until softened, about 3 minutes. Drain the tomatoes, reserving 1 to 2 tablespoons of the liquid. Coarsely chop the tomatoes.

Make the salsa. In a blender or food processor fitted with a steel blade, add the sun-dried tomatoes, reserved liquid, fresh tomato, onion, scallions, cilantro, garlic, vinegar, oil, salt, and pepper and process for 3 to 4 seconds. Transfer to a small bowl.

Warm the flour tortillas over a hot burner or in a skillet and place on serving plates. Spoon the rice over one-half of each tortilla. Top each with the beans, salsa, and yogurt. Fold the remaining half of the tortillas over and press down lightly. Serve the quesadillas immediately.

Makes 6 servings

Per serving:
298 Calories; 10g Protein; 3g Fat; 59g Carbohydrates; 1mg Cholesterol; 775mg Sodium; 9g Fiber

Baked Vegetable Pie with Masa Crust

2 cups masa harina (see Helpful Hints, page 57)
2 cups low-fat milk or soy milk
½ teaspoon turmeric
2 teaspoons canola oil
1 medium yellow onion, diced
1 green bell pepper, seeded and diced
1 small zucchini, diced
One 15-ounce can crushed tomatoes
One 11-ounce can corn kernels, drained
1 tablespoon commercial taco seasoning (see Helpful Hint, page 19)
⅓ cup shredded low-fat Swiss or cheddar cheese

Preheat the oven to 400°F.

In a mixing bowl, combine the masa harina, milk, and turmeric and blend into a moist dough. Spread the dough onto two lightly greased 9-inch pie pans, using the back of a spoon to spread the dough evenly over the bottoms and up the sides of the pans. Bake until the crust is dry, 12 to 14 minutes. Remove from the oven.

Meanwhile, in a large saucepan, heat the oil over medium heat. Add the onion, bell pepper, and zucchini and cook over medium heat, stirring, until the vegetables are tender, about 7 minutes. Stir in the crushed tomatoes, corn, and taco seasoning and bring to a simmer. Cook for 10 minutes over medium-low heat, stirring occasionally.

When the crusts are ready, ladle the vegetable mixture over the top of each crust. Sprinkle with cheese and place in the oven. Bake until the cheese is melted, about 5 minutes. Remove from the heat and cut each pie into 4 wedges. Use a wide spatula to transfer the pie pieces to serving plates.

Makes 6 to 8 servings

Per serving:
291 Calories; 11g Protein; 5g Fat; 56g Carbohydrates; 9mg Cholesterol; 254mg Sodium; 6g Fiber

Black Bean and Rice Flautas

Flautas are simple, tightly rolled, flute-shaped burritos that are typically fried. This healthful variation skips the frying step.

1 cup white rice
3 cups water
2 teaspoons canola oil
1 small yellow onion, chopped
1 cup mince-style TVP (textured
    vegetable protein)
1½ tablespoons commercial
    taco seasoning (see Helpful
    Hint, page 19)
One 15-ounce can black beans,
    drained
Six 7-inch flour tortillas
¾ cup tomato salsa
¾ cup guacamole (optional)

In a medium saucepan, combine the rice and 2 cups water and bring to a simmer. Stir the rice, cover, and cook over medium-low heat, until tender, 12 to 15 minutes. Fluff the grains with a fork and let stand, covered, for 5 minutes.

In another medium saucepan, heat the oil over medium heat. Add the onion and cook, stirring, until tender, about 4 minutes. Add the remaining 1 cup water, TVP, and taco seasoning and bring to a simmer. Cook, stirring, about 5 minutes. Add the beans and cook, stirring, for 5 minutes. Fold in the cooked rice and blend thoroughly.

Warm the tortillas over a hot burner or in a skillet and place on serving plates. Spoon the bean and rice mixture down the center of each tortilla and top with the salsa and guacamole if desired. Roll the tortillas tightly around the filling. Serve at once.

**Makes 6 flautas
(6 servings)**

Per serving:
301 Calories; 19g Protein; 3g Fat;
57g Carbohydrates; 0 Cholesterol;
1,268mg Sodium; 14g Fiber

Quick Bean Tacos

**One 15-ounce can black
beans or pinto beans,
undrained**
2 teaspoons canola oil
1 small yellow onion, diced
**1 tablespoon commercial taco
seasoning (see Helpful Hint,
page 19)**
6 taco shells
**6 to 8 leaves romaine lettuce,
cut into strips**
**1 cup tomato salsa or taco
sauce**
**6 tablespoons shredded low-fat
Monterey Jack cheese**

Preheat the oven to 350°F.

Drain the beans, reserving
¼ cup of the liquid. In a medium saucepan, heat the oil over
medium heat. Add the onion and
cook, stirring, until tender, about

4 minutes. Add the beans, reserved liquid, and taco seasoning
and cook, stirring, until beans are
heated through, about 6 minutes.
Transfer three-quarters of the
beans to a blender or food processor fitted with a steel blade
and process until smooth, about
5 seconds, stopping to stir at least
once. Return the beans to the pan
and cook over low heat, stirring,
until heated through, about 5
minutes.

Meanwhile, arrange the taco
shells on a large baking pan. Bake
5 to 6 minutes. Remove from the
oven and place on a serving
platter.

Fill the tacos with 3 to 4 tablespoons of the beans. Top with the
greens, salsa, and cheese. Serve
immediately.

**Makes 6 tacos
(3 servings)**

VARIATIONS

*Other taco fillings include chopped
scallions, pickled jalapeños,
and/or guacamole.*

Per serving:
154 Calories; 6g Protein; 6g Fat;
22g Carbohydrates; 5mg Cholesterol; 856mg Sodium; 7g Fiber

Pasta with Spicy Pipian Sauce

Pipian *refers to a ground paste of pumpkin seeds and spices.*
Here, it inspires a nutty-textured sauce for pasta.

1 tablespoon olive oil
1 medium yellow onion, diced
2 large cloves garlic, minced
One 28-ounce can plum
  tomatoes, undrained
½ cup toasted pumpkin seeds
  (see Pepitas, page 13)
¼ cup chopped fresh parsley
1 tablespoon chopped pickled
  jalapeños
2 teaspoons dried oregano
1 teaspoon ground cumin
½ teaspoon freshly ground
  black pepper
½ teaspoon salt
8 ounces thin spaghetti or
  vermicelli

In a large saucepan, heat the oil over medium heat. Add the onion and garlic and cook, stirring, until the onion is translucent, about 4 minutes. Add the plum tomatoes and liquid, pumpkin seeds, parsley, jalapeños, and seasonings and bring to a simmer. Cook for 15 to 20 minutes over low heat, stirring occasionally.

Transfer the sauce to a blender or food processor fitted with a steel blade and process until smooth, about 5 seconds. Return to the pan and keep warm.

Meanwhile, in a medium saucepan, bring 3 quarts of water to a boil over medium-high heat. Place the noodles in the boiling water, stir, and return to a boil. Cook over medium-high heat until *al dente,* 6 to 8 minutes, stirring occasionally. Drain in a colander.

Place the noodles on serving plates and ladle the sauce over the top.

Makes 4 servings

Per serving:
234 Calories; 12g Protein; 10g Fat;
15g Carbohydrates; 0 Cholesterol;
723mg Sodium; 3g Fiber

Black Bean Posole

This hearty chili-like stew can be made spicier by adding bottled hot sauce or chopped jalapeños to the pot.

1 tablespoon canola oil
1 medium yellow onion, diced
1 green bell pepper, seeded
    and diced
2 ribs celery, chopped
2 cloves garlic, minced
One 28-ounce can tomato puree
One 15-ounce can black beans,
    drained
One 14-ounce can hominy corn,
    drained
½ cup water
1 tablespoon dried oregano
1 tablespoon chili powder
½ teaspoon salt
½ teaspoon freshly ground
    black pepper

In a large saucepan, heat the oil over medium-high heat. Add the onion, bell pepper, celery, and garlic and cook, stirring, until tender, 5 to 7 minutes. Stir in the remaining ingredients and bring to a simmer. Reduce heat to medium-low and cook for 15 minutes, stirring occasionally. Remove from the heat and let stand for 5 minutes before serving.

Ladle the *posole* into bowls and serve with warm flour tortillas. You can also serve the *posole* over rice or other grains.

Makes 4 servings

Per serving:
243 Calories; 9g Protein; 4g Fat;
49g Carbohydrates; 0 Cholesterol;
1,659mg Sodium; 12g Fiber

Curried Potato and Chickpea "Wrap"

Curried vegetables form a delectable filling for this cross-cultural creation.
Soothing yogurt fills the role typically occupied by salsa.

1 tablespoon canola oil
1 small yellow onion, diced
2 large carrots, peeled and
diced
4 cloves garlic, minced
1 tablespoon chopped pickled
jalapeños (optional)
1 tablespoon curry powder
½ teaspoon salt
¼ teaspoon cayenne pepper
4 cups diced white potatoes
3 cups water
One 15-ounce can chickpeas,
drained
4 whole scallions, trimmed
and chopped
Four 10-inch flour tortillas
1 cup low-fat plain yogurt

In a large saucepan, heat the oil over medium-high heat. Add the onion, carrots, and garlic and cook, stirring frequently, until onion is tender, about 5 minutes. Add the jalapeños if desired, curry powder, salt, and cayenne and cook, stirring, for 30 seconds. Stir in the potatoes and water and bring to a simmer. Cook over medium heat until the potatoes and carrots are tender, about 15 minutes. Stir in the chickpeas and scallions and cook, stirring, 3 to 4 minutes. To thicken, mash the potatoes against the side of the pan with a spoon.

Meanwhile, warm the flour tortillas over a hot burner or in a skillet and place on large serving plates. Spoon the potato mixture down the center of the tortillas. Roll the tortillas around the filling, creating burritos. Spoon the yogurt on the side of the burritos.

Makes 4 wraps
(4 servings)

Per serving:
526 Calories; 16g Protein; 8g Fat; 100g Carbohydrates; 3mg Cholesterol; 803mg Sodium; 12g Fiber

Spinach Rice and Beans

Here's an enticing variation of the classic combination of rice and beans.
For a twist, use an aromatic grain such as basmati or jasmine rice.

1 tablespoon canola oil
1 medium yellow onion, diced
2 large cloves garlic, minced
4 to 5 cups coarsely chopped
  fresh spinach
½ teaspoon turmeric
½ teaspoon salt
½ teaspoon freshly ground
  black pepper
3 cups water
1½ cups basmati, jasmine, or
  long-grain white rice
1 cup canned pink beans or
  cranberry beans (see
  Helpful Hints, page 106)

In a large saucepan, heat the oil over medium heat. Add the onion and garlic and cook, stirring, until tender, about 4 minutes. Stir in the spinach, turmeric, salt, and pepper and cook, stirring, until the greens are wilted, about 4 minutes. Stir in the water, rice, and beans and bring to a simmer. Reduce heat to medium-low, cover, and cook until all of the liquid is absorbed, 15 to 20 minutes.

Fluff the rice with a fork and let stand for 5 to 10 minutes (still covered) before serving.

Makes 6 servings

Per serving:
232 Calories; 7g Protein; 4g Fat;
45g Carbohydrates; 0 Cholesterol;
225mg Sodium; 5g Fiber

Chayote Vegetable Stew

The firm texture of chayote makes it a favorite ingredient for well-simmered stews and soups. This soup takes a little more than 30 minutes to prepare, but it is time well spent.

1 tablespoon canola oil
1 medium yellow onion, diced
1 green bell pepper, seeded and diced
2 chayotes, seeded and diced (see Helpful Hints, page 57)
3 cups vegetable broth
1 large white potato, diced
1 large carrot, peeled and diced
½ teaspoon salt
½ teaspoon freshly ground black pepper
1 cup cooked chickpeas
¼ cup minced fresh parsley

In a large saucepan, heat the oil over medium heat. Add the onion, bell pepper, and chayotes and cook, stirring, about 8 minutes. Add the vegetable broth, potato, carrot, and seasonings and bring to a simmer. Cook over medium-low heat until the potato and chayotes are tender, 20 to 25 minutes, stirring occasionally. Stir in the chickpeas and parsley and cook for another 5 minutes.

Ladle the stew into wide bowls and serve with a grain such as rice, couscous, or quinoa.

Makes 4 servings

Per serving:
173 Calories; 6g Protein; 7g Fat;
25g Carbohydrates; 0 Cholesterol;
1,151mg Sodium; 4g Fiber

Jicama Quesadillas

Four 10-inch flour tortillas
1 cup peeled and diced jicama
1 cup cooked corn kernels
1 cup jarred roasted red
peppers, cut into strips
3 to 4 whole scallions, trimmed
and chopped
2 tablespoons pickled jalapeño
slices (optional)
½ to 1 cup tomato salsa
½ cup shredded low-fat
Monterey Jack or Swiss
cheese

Preheat the broiler.

Arrange the tortillas on two sheet pans. Fill the center of each flat tortilla with ¼ cup each of jicama, corn, and bell peppers, forming small mounds. Sprinkle the scallions and jalapeños if desired over the top and follow with about 2 tablespoons salsa and cheese. Broil until the cheese is melted, 2 to 3 minutes. Remove from the heat and fold the tortillas over the fillings, forming pockets. Using a wide spatula, transfer the quesadillas to serving plates and serve at once.

Makes 4 quesadillas
(4 servings)

Per serving:
229 Calories; 10g Protein; 4g Fat; 40g Carbohydrates; 10mg Cholesterol; 873mg Sodium; 14g Fiber

Herb Potato and Carrot Burritos

A burrito for the potato lovers of the world.

**3 cups peeled and diced white
 potatoes**
3 to 4 carrots, peeled and diced
1 tablespoon canola oil
**1 medium yellow onion,
 chopped**
2 cloves garlic, minced
**One 15-ounce can corn kernels,
 drained**
¼ cup chopped fresh parsley
2 teaspoons dried oregano
1 teaspoon paprika
½ teaspoon dried thyme
½ teaspoon salt
**½ teaspoon freshly ground
 black pepper**
Four 10-inch flour tortillas
½ cup low-fat plain yogurt
Taco sauce or salsa (optional)

Place the potatoes and carrots in boiling water to cover and cook over medium heat until tender, about 15 minutes. Drain in a colander.

In a large saucepan, heat the oil over medium-high heat. Add the onion and garlic, and cook, stirring, until tender, about 5 minutes. Stir in the potatoes, carrots, corn, parsley, oregano, paprika, thyme, salt, and pepper and cook, stirring, until corn is heated through, 5 to 6 minutes.

Meanwhile, warm the flour tortillas over a hot burner or in a skillet and place on large serving plates. Spoon the potato mixture down the center of the tortillas. Spoon about 2 tablespoons of yogurt over the top of each filling. Roll the tortillas around the filling, creating burritos. If desired, serve with taco sauce or salsa.

**Makes 4 burritos
(4 servings)**

Per serving:
375 Calories, 10g Protein; 7g Fat;
72g Carbohydrates; 1mg Cholesterol; 710mg Sodium; 7g Fiber

Serrano Rice and Beans

*In this authentic dish, several whole serrano chilies are simmered with
the rice and then removed at the finish. The chilies can be served
on the side for those who love hot peppers.*

1 tablespoon canola oil
1 medium yellow onion, diced
1 green bell pepper, seeded
   and diced
2 large cloves garlic, minced
One 14-ounce can stewed
   tomatoes, drained
4 to 6 serrano chilies, left whole
2 teaspoons dried oregano
½ teaspoon turmeric
½ teaspoon salt
½ teaspoon freshly ground
   black pepper
3 cups water
1½ cups long-grain white rice
1 cup cooked black beans or
   pinto beans, drained

In a large saucepan, heat the oil
over medium heat. Add the onion,
bell pepper, and garlic and cook,
stirring, until tender, about
5 minutes. Stir in the tomatoes,
chilies, oregano, turmeric, salt,
and pepper and cook, stirring, for
2 minutes. Stir in the water, rice,
and beans and bring to a simmer.
Cover and cook over medium-low
heat until all of the liquid is
absorbed, 15 to 20 minutes.

Fluff the rice with a fork and
let stand for 5 minutes, covered,
before serving.

Makes 6 servings

Per serving:
142 Calories; 5g Protein; 3g Fat;
25g Carbohydrates; 0 Cholesterol;
320mg Sodium; 4g Fiber

Festive Burrito with Avocado, Rice, and Bell Peppers

Ripe avocados, roasted red peppers, and pinto beans combine with yellow rice to form a multicolored filling for this tasty burrito.

2 cups water
1 cup white rice
½ teaspoon turmeric
½ teaspoon salt
½ teaspoon freshly ground black pepper
One 15-ounce can pinto beans, drained and warmed
½ cup jarred roasted red peppers, diced
1 ripe avocado, peeled, pitted, and diced (see Helpful Hints, page 11)
2 whole scallions, trimmed and chopped
Four 10-inch flour tortillas
½ cup tomato salsa

In a medium saucepan, combine the water, rice, turmeric, salt, and pepper. Bring to a simmer; reduce heat to medium-low, stir the rice, cover the pan, and cook until water is absorbed, 12 to 15 minutes. Remove from heat, fluff the grains with a fork, and fold in the beans, bell peppers, avocado, and scallions. Let stand, still covered, for 5 to 10 minutes.

Warm the tortillas over a hot burner or in a skillet and place on large serving plates. Spoon the rice mixture down the center of each tortilla. Roll the tortillas around the filling, creating burritos. Spoon the salsa on the side of the burritos and serve at once.

**Makes 4 burritos
(4 servings)**

Per serving:
412 Calories; 11g Protein; 8g Fat; 72g Carbohydrates; 0 Cholesterol; 1,383mg Sodium; 18g Fiber

Aztec Quinoa Stew

Quinoa is a tiny, nutty grain that cooks up like rice. Although quinoa is better known for its South American ancestry, the grain also has roots in ancient Mexican cultures.

1 tablespoon canola oil
1 medium yellow onion, diced
1 red or green bell pepper,
   seeded and diced
3 to 4 cloves garlic, minced
4 cups chopped fresh spinach
2½ cups water or vegetable
   broth
1 large white potato, peeled
   and diced
1 cup quinoa, rinsed
1 tablespoon dried parsley
1 teaspoon dried oregano
½ teaspoon salt
½ teaspoon freshly ground
   black pepper
One 15-ounce can corn kernels,
   drained

In a large saucepan, heat the oil over medium-high heat. Add the onion, bell pepper, and garlic and cook, stirring, until tender, about 5 minutes. Stir in the spinach and cook, stirring, until the leaves are wilted, about 2 minutes. Add the water, potato, quinoa, parsley, oregano, salt, and pepper and bring to a simmer. Cook over medium-low heat for 12 minutes, stirring occasionally. Stir in the corn and cook until the potatoes are tender, about 5 minutes.

Ladle the stew into bowls and serve with warm flour tortillas.

Makes 4 servings

Per serving:
300 Calories; 10g Protein; 7g Fat;
54g Carbohydrates; 0 Cholesterol;
546mg Sodium; 7g Fiber

CHAPTER 4

Side Dishes

Cilantro-Spiced Black Beans

*In a matter of minutes, canned black beans are
transformed into a savory side dish.*

**Two 15-ounce cans black beans,
undrained**
**3 to 4 whole scallions, trimmed
and chopped**
**1½ tablespoons commercial
taco seasoning (see Helpful
Hint, page 19)**
**½ teaspoon freshly ground
black pepper**
**3 to 4 tablespoons chopped
cilantro**

Drain the beans, reserving ½ cup
of the liquid. Add the beans,
reserved liquid, scallions, taco
seasoning, and black pepper to a
medium saucepan. Cook over
medium heat, stirring, until
heated through, about 10 minutes.
Mash the beans against the side of
the pan with the back of a spoon
while they cook. Remove from the
heat and blend in the cilantro.

Serve the beans as a side dish to
burritos, rice dishes, or pilafs.

Makes 6 servings

Per serving:
152 Calories; 9g Protein; 0.4g Fat;
28g Carbohydrates; 0 Cholesterol;
2mg Sodium; 6g Fiber

Asparagus with Lime-Cilantro Vinaigrette

*Asparagus, the regal vegetable, is coated with a light citrus dressing.
Cilantro—the parsley of Mexico—provides an herbal tang.*

Juice of 1 lime
2 tablespoons olive oil
**2 to 3 tablespoons chopped
  cilantro**
1 to 2 cloves garlic, minced
½ teaspoon salt
½ teaspoon white pepper
**½ cup jarred roasted red
  peppers, chopped**
**1¼ pounds asparagus spears,
  fibrous ends removed**

In small mixing bowl, whisk together the lime juice, olive oil, cilantro, garlic, salt, and white pepper. Stir in the roasted red peppers and set aside. (This can be made several hours ahead of time and refrigerated.)

Bring about 1 quart of water to a boil in a medium saucepan. Place the asparagus in the boiling water and cook over medium heat until tender, 3 to 4 minutes. Drain in a colander. (Alternatively, steam the asparagus until tender.)

In a large mixing bowl, gently toss the asparagus with the lime-cilantro dressing. Arrange the asparagus spears on a platter and serve as a side dish.

Makes 4 servings

Per serving:
67 Calories; 2g Protein; 5g Fat;
4g Carbohydrates; 0 Cholesterol;
183mg Sodium; 2g Fiber

Tomatillo Pilaf

Tomatillos add a tangy flavor to this herb-scented rice dish. When combined with refried beans, this pilaf can also be used as a filling for burritos.

1 tablespoon canola oil
1 medium yellow onion, diced
1 green bell pepper, seeded
   and diced
6 fresh tomatillos, husks
   removed, diced
3 to 4 whole scallions, trimmed
   and chopped
2 teaspoons dried oregano
1 teaspoon ground cumin
½ teaspoon turmeric
½ teaspoon salt
½ teaspoon freshly ground
   black pepper
2½ cups water
1¼ cups long-grain white rice

In a large saucepan, heat the oil over medium heat. Add the onion and bell pepper and cook, stirring, until tender, about 4 minutes. Add the tomatillos, scallions, oregano, cumin, turmeric, salt, and pepper and cook, stirring, for 3 minutes. Stir in the water and rice and bring to a simmer. Reduce heat to medium-low, cover, and cook until all of the liquid is absorbed, 15 to 20 minutes.

Fluff the rice with a fork and let stand for 5 to 10 minutes, covered, before serving as a side dish.

Makes 4 servings

Per serving:
284 Calories; 5g Protein; 4g Fat;
55g Carbohydrates; 0 Cholesterol;
283mg Sodium; 3g Fiber

Braised Carrots and Nopales with Balsamic Vinaigrette

Serve this side dish to family or guests and you will never be accused of serving the "same-old, same-old."

2 large nopales (see Helpful Hint, page 33)
3 to 4 carrots, peeled and cut into ¼-inch matchsticks
2 tablespoons balsamic vinegar
2 tablespoons chopped fresh parsley
1 tablespoon honey
1 tablespoon canola oil
1 teaspoon Dijon-style mustard
½ teaspoon salt
½ teaspoon freshly ground black pepper
2 teaspoons sesame seeds

To prepare the nopales, scrape off the prickly needles and bumps where the needles grew. Cut off the base and trim around the outer edge of the paddle. Cut the paddles in half crosswise, then cut into ¼-inch-wide strips. The strips should resemble green beans.

In a medium saucepan, bring 2 inches of water (about 1½ cups) to a boil. Place the carrots and nopales strips in the boiling water and cover. Cook over medium heat until the vegetables are tender, stirring occasionally, 10 to 12 minutes. Drain in a colander.

Meanwhile, in a medium mixing bowl, combine the vinegar, parsley, honey, oil, mustard, salt, and pepper and whisk together. Blend in the carrots and nopales and let stand for 5 minutes to allow the flavors to meld.

Using a slotted spoon, arrange the vegetables on a platter. Sprinkle the sesame seeds over the top.

Makes 4 servings

Helpful Hint

Leftovers can be chilled and served as a salad.

Per serving:
103 Calories; 2g Protein; 5g Fat; 14g Carbohydrates; 0 Cholesterol; 325mg Sodium; 3g Fiber

Jalapeño–Sesame Seed Corn Bread

Chopped jalapeño peppers deliver a kick to this spicy corn bread.

1 cup yellow cornmeal
1 cup unbleached all-purpose
  flour
⅓ cup sugar
1 tablespoon baking powder
½ teaspoon salt
1 large egg plus 1 large egg
  white, beaten
1 cup low-fat milk or soy milk
3 tablespoons canola oil
One 11-ounce can corn kernels,
  drained
2 to 3 tablespoons chopped
  pickled jalapeños
¼ cup roasted sesame seeds

Preheat the oven to 375°F.

Combine the cornmeal, flour, sugar, baking powder, and salt in a mixing bowl. In a separate bowl, whisk together the eggs, milk, and oil. Gently fold the liquid ingredients into the dry ingredients until a batter is formed. Fold in the corn and jalapeños.

Pour the batter into a lightly greased 8-inch square baking pan. Sprinkle the sesame seeds evenly over the top. Bake until the crust is light brown and a toothpick inserted in the center comes out clean, 20 to 25 minutes. Remove from the heat and let cool for a few minutes before cutting into pieces. Serve warm.

Makes 8 servings

Per serving:
277 Calories; 7g Protein; 9g Fat; 43g Carbohydrates; 28mg Cholesterol; 485mg Sodium; 3g Fiber

Olla Frijoles

ONE-POT BEANS

The term olla frijoles *loosely means "pot beans." Although traditional recipes call for cooking dried beans from scratch, this quick version takes advantage of canned beans.*

One 15-ounce can pinto beans
One 15-ounce can black beans
1 tablespoon canola oil
1 large yellow onion, diced
1 red bell pepper, seeded
   and diced
2 ribs celery, chopped
3 to 4 cloves garlic, minced
1 tablespoon chopped pickled
   jalapeños
¼ cup chopped fresh parsley
1 tablespoon dried oregano
1 teaspoon ground cumin
½ teaspoon salt
½ teaspoon freshly ground
   black pepper

Drain the beans, reserving ½ cup of the liquid.

In a large saucepan, heat the oil over medium heat. Add the onion, bell pepper, celery, garlic, and jalapeños and cook, stirring, until tender, about 5 minutes. Add the beans, reserved liquid, parsley, oregano, cumin, salt, and pepper and bring to a simmer. Lower the heat to medium-low and cook for about 15 minutes, stirring occasionally.

To thicken, add about half of the bean mixture to a blender or food processor fitted with a steel blade and process until smooth, about 5 seconds; return bean mixture to the pan. Keep warm until ready to serve. For an authentic presentation, serve the beans in a ceramic bowl or terra-cotta pot.

Makes 6 servings

Per serving:
122 Calories; 6g Protein; 3g Fat; 22g Carbohydrates; 0 Cholesterol; 740mg Sodium; 6g Fiber

Lime-Braised Greens and Corn

In this simple and nutritious dish, a squeeze of lime enhances
the mellow flavors of braised greens and corn.

**1 large bunch kale or field
   spinach**
1 tablespoon canola oil
**One 15-ounce can corn kernels,
   drained**
**1 medium yellow onion, finely
   chopped**
**2 cloves garlic, minced
   (optional)**
Juice of 1 lime
½ teaspoon salt
**½ teaspoon freshly ground
   black pepper**

Place the greens in a colander and
rinse under cold running water.
Remove the stems and coarsely
chop the leaves.

In a large saucepan, heat the oil
over medium heat. Add the corn,
onion, and garlic if desired, and
cook, stirring, until tender, about
4 minutes. Add the greens, lime
juice, salt, and pepper and cook
until the greens are wilted, about
4 minutes. Serve immediately.

Makes 4 servings

Per serving:
166 Calories; 5g Protein; 5g Fat;
24g Carbohydrates; 0 Cholesterol;
611mg Sodium; 5g Fiber

Poblano Rice with Artichokes

This savory pilaf-style dish is filled with green vegetables, artichokes, and roasted chilies.

2 to 3 poblano chilies, cored
    and seeded
1 tablespoon canola oil
1 medium yellow onion, diced
8 ounces fresh white mush-
    rooms, chopped
3 to 4 cloves garlic, minced
2½ cups chopped fresh spinach
3¼ cups water
One 14-ounce can artichoke
    hearts, drained and
    coarsely chopped
1½ cups long-grain white rice
1½ teaspoons ground cumin
1 teaspoon salt
½ teaspoon freshly ground
    black pepper
¼ cup chopped fresh parsley
4 whole scallions, trimmed
    and chopped
Juice of 1 lime

Preheat the broiler.

Arrange the chilies on a cookie sheet. Place the pan under the broiler and broil until the skins are slightly charred all over, 4 to 5 minutes on each side. Remove from the heat and let cool for a few minutes. With a butter knife (or your hands—use rubber gloves to protect your skin), peel off the charred skin and discard. Finely chop the flesh.

Meanwhile, in a medium saucepan, heat the oil over medium heat. Add the onion, mushrooms, and garlic and cook, stirring, until tender, about 5 minutes. Stir in the spinach and cook, stirring, until the leaves are wilted, about 2 minutes. Stir in the water, artichokes, rice, cumin, salt, pepper, and chopped chilies and bring to a simmer. Cover and cook over medium-low heat until all of the liquid is absorbed, about 20 minutes.

When the rice is done, fluff the grains with a fork and fold in the parsley, scallions, and lime juice. Let stand, covered, for about 5 minutes before serving.

Makes 6 servings

Per serving:
208 Calories; 6g Protein; 3g Fat;
40g Carbohydrates; 0 Cholesterol;
523mg Sodium; 3g Fiber

Chipotle Mashed Potatoes

Chipotle peppers enliven a bowl of mashed potatoes with a smoky heat.

2 large white potatoes, peeled and diced
1 to 2 canned chipotle chilies, seeds removed
2 cloves garlic, chopped
½ cup hot whole milk or soy milk
2 tablespoons butter, softened (optional)
2 tablespoons chopped fresh parsley
1 teaspoon paprika
½ teaspoon salt

Helpful Hints

The potatoes also can be mashed by hand with a potato masher. Remember to mince the chipotle pepper and garlic ahead of time.

In a medium saucepan, bring about 2 quarts of water to a boil. Place the potatoes in boiling water and cook, over medium heat, stirring occasionally, until the potatoes are easily pierced with a fork, about 20 minutes. Drain the potatoes in a colander.

To a blender or food processor fitted with a steel blade, add the chipotle peppers and garlic and process until minced, about 5 seconds. Add the potatoes, milk, butter if desired, parsley, paprika, and salt and process until the mixture is smooth, about 10 seconds. Stop to scrape the sides at least once. (Leave a few lumps for a "home-style" texture.)

Transfer the potatoes to a bowl and serve immediately.

Makes 4 servings

Per serving:
105 Calories; 2g Protein; 1g Fat; 21g Carbohydrates; 4mg Cholesterol; 274mg Sodium; 2g Fiber

Borracho Pinto Beans

"DRUNKEN" BEANS

Borracho refers to dishes that have been cooked with beer or liquor. (The term borracho *means "drunken.") If you like the taste of beer, you'll like this mischievous dish.*

1 tablespoon canola oil
1 medium yellow onion, chopped
1 red bell pepper, seeded and diced
2 large cloves garlic, minced
1 jalapeño pepper, seeded and minced (optional)
Two 15-ounce cans pinto beans, drained
½ cup stale beer (not foamy)
1 tablespoon dried parsley
1 teaspoon ground cumin
½ teaspoon freshly ground black pepper
2 tablespoons chopped cilantro

In a medium saucepan, heat the oil over medium heat. Add the onion, bell pepper, garlic, and jalapeño if desired and cook, stirring, until tender, about 5 minutes. Stir in the beans, beer, parsley, cumin, and pepper and cook over medium-low heat for 8 to 10 minutes, stirring frequently.

Remove the beans from the heat and blend in the cilantro. If desired, transfer half of the bean mixture to a blender or a food processor fitted with a steel blade and process until smooth, about 5 seconds. Return to the pan.

Serve the beans as a side dish or as a filling for quesadillas.

Makes 4 servings

Per serving:
201 Calories; 9g Protein; 4g Fat; 32g Carbohydrates; 0 Cholesterol; 751mg Sodium; 7g Fiber

Mashed Calabaza

A variety of hard-shelled squash and pumpkin (called calabaza*) are harvested throughout Mexico. Small varieties of winter squash have soft textures and sweet flavors and bake in less than 30 minutes.*

3 to 4 delicata squash, sweet dumpling, or other small winter squash
½ cup whole milk or soy milk
1 to 2 tablespoons maple syrup
¼ teaspoon ground cinnamon or nutmeg
¼ teaspoon white pepper

Preheat the oven to 400°F.

Cut the squash in half lengthwise and scoop out the seeds and stringy fibers. Place the squash cut-side down on a baking sheet with sides that is filled with about ¼-inch water. Bake until the flesh is tender (easily pierced with a fork), 20 to 25 minutes. Remove the squash from the oven, flip over, and let cool for a few minutes.

When the squash has cooled, scoop out the pulp and transfer to medium mixing bowl. Add the milk, maple syrup, cinnamon, and white pepper and mash like potatoes. Serve immediately.

Makes 4 servings

Per serving:
114 Calories; 3g Protein; 1g Fat; 24g Carbohydrates; 4mg Cholesterol; 9mg Sodium; 6g Fiber

Mexican Rice and Peas

This versatile side dish can accompany almost any Mexican meal.

1 tablespoon canola oil
1 medium yellow onion, diced
1 green bell pepper, seeded
**   and diced**
2 large cloves garlic, minced
One 14-ounce can stewed
**   tomatoes, drained**
2 teaspoons dried oregano
½ teaspoon turmeric
½ teaspoon salt
½ teaspoon freshly ground
**   black pepper**
3 cups water
1½ cups long-grain white rice
1 cup frozen green peas

In a large saucepan, heat the oil over medium heat. Add the onion, bell pepper, and garlic and cook, stirring, until tender, about 5 minutes. Stir in the tomatoes, oregano, turmeric, salt, and pepper and cook for 2 minutes. Stir in the water, rice, and peas and bring to a simmer. Reduce heat to medium-low, cover, and cook until all of the liquid is absorbed, about 20 minutes.

Fluff the rice with a fork and let stand for 5 to 10 minutes, covered, before serving.

Makes 6 servings

Per serving:
212 Calories; 5g Protein; 3g Fat;
41g Carbohydrates; 0 Cholesterol;
356mg Sodium; 3g Fiber

Skillet Nopalitos with Onion and Tomatoes

Ready-to-use and precooked nopalitos (small cactus paddles) are sold in water-packed jars. Precooked nopalitos are a boon to the adventurous cook who is pressed for time.

2 teaspoons canola oil
1 medium yellow onion,
  thinly sliced
2 to 3 cloves garlic, minced
2 cups jarred nopalitos, rinsed
  and cut into strips (see
  Helpful Hint, page 68)
2 tomatoes, diced
2 teaspoons dried oregano
½ teaspoon freshly ground
  black pepper

In a medium saucepan, heat the oil over medium heat. Add the onion and garlic, and cook, stirring, until the onion is translucent, about 4 minutes. Add the nopalitos, tomatoes, oregano, and pepper, and cook, stirring, until the tomatoes are thick and saucelike, about 10 minutes. Remove the pan from the heat. Serve immediately.

Makes 4 servings

Per serving:
75 Calories; 2g Protein; 3g Fat; 11g Carbohydrates; 0 Cholesterol; 435mg Sodium; 4g Fiber

Double Corn Griddle Cakes

Here's another imaginative way to use corn, one of Mexico's most cherished crops. Serve these pancakes either as an appetizer or entrée at a Mexican-themed brunch.

¾ cup cornmeal
½ cup unbleached all-purpose
   flour
2 tablespoons sugar
1 teaspoon salt
1 teaspoon baking powder
1 large egg, beaten
2 tablespoons canola oil
1 cup buttermilk or low-fat milk
One 11-ounce can corn kernels,
   drained
2 whole scallions, trimmed and
   chopped
½ teaspoon freshly ground
   black pepper
Salsa or taco sauce (optional)

Combine the dry ingredients in a medium mixing bowl. In a separate bowl, whisk together the egg, oil, and buttermilk. Fold the liquid ingredients into the dry ingredients, forming a batter. Blend in the corn, scallions, and black pepper.

Preheat a lightly greased nonstick griddle or skillet over medium-high heat. Spoon about ½ cup of the batter onto the hot surface. Cook the pancake until the edges and underside are light brown, about 4 minutes. (It's okay to peek.) Gently flip the pancake and continue cooking until the remaining side is light brown, about 2 minutes. Remove to a warm plate.

Reduce the heat to medium and repeat the process with the remaining batter. Stack the finished pancakes and cover with waxed paper. If desired, serve with salsa or taco sauce.

Makes about 6 pancakes

Per pancake:
209 Calories, 6g Protein; 6g Fat; 33g Carbohydrates; 36mg Cholesterol; 510mg Sodium; 2g Fiber

Zucchini and Pink Bean Succotash

*Here is a south-of-the-border spin on succotash,
the classic combination of beans and corn.*

2 teaspoons canola oil
1 medium zucchini, diced
1 small yellow onion, diced
**One 15-ounce can pink beans or
  pinto beans, drained**
**One 15-ounce can corn kernels,
  drained**
**½ cup jarred roasted red
  peppers, diced**
½ teaspoon salt
**½ teaspoon freshly ground
  black pepper**

In a medium saucepan, heat the
oil over medium heat. Add the
zucchini and onion and cook,
stirring, until the zucchini is
tender, 6 to 7 minutes. Add the
beans, corn, roasted peppers, salt,
and pepper and cook, stirring,
until the vegetables are steaming,
about 5 minutes.

Makes 6 servings

VARIATIONS

*For calabacitas succotash, use 6 to
8 baby zucchini or baby pattypan
squash (halved) in place
of the zucchini.*

Per serving:
170 Calories; 6g Protein; 2g Fat;
32g Carbohydrates; 0 Cholesterol;
374mg Sodium; 7g Fiber

Roasted Sweet Plátanos

Although plátanos, *or plantains, are typically fried, roasting is a healthier way to enjoy these "vegetable bananas." Remember: Ripe, yellowish plantains are sweeter (and more desirable to the gringo palate) than the hard, green varieties.*

4 ripe yellow plantains
¼ teaspoon ground nutmeg
or cinnamon

Preheat the oven to 400°F.

Cut off the tips of the plantains. Place the plantains on a baking sheet and bake until the outer skin is charred and puffy and the flesh is tender, 15 to 20 minutes. Remove from oven and let cool for a few minutes.

Slice the plantains down the center lengthwise and peel back the skin. Cut the plantains in half crosswise, sprinkle with nutmeg or cinnamon, and transfer to serving plates.

Makes 4 to 6 servings

Helpful Hints

If the plantains are green, store them at room temperature for 5 to 7 days until they ripen to yellow. Placing the plantains in a paper bag will expedite the process (but do not refrigerate).

Per serving:
219 Calories; 2g Protein; 0.4g Fat; 51g Carbohydrates; 0 Cholesterol; 7mg Sodium; 4g Fiber

Green Rice with Winter Squash

Called arroz verde, *this pilaf-style dish is chock full of nourishing ingredients and flavors.*

1 tablespoon canola oil
1 medium yellow onion, diced
1 green bell pepper, seeded
　　and diced
3 to 4 cloves garlic, minced
1 large jalapeño pepper, seeded
　　and minced (optional)
2½ cups chopped fresh spinach
　　or kale
3½ cups water
2 cups peeled and diced
　　butternut squash
1½ cups long-grain white rice
4 whole scallions, chopped
¼ cup chopped fresh parsley
1½ teaspoons ground cumin
1 teaspoon salt
½ teaspoon freshly ground
　　black pepper

In a medium saucepan, heat the oil over medium heat. Add the onion, bell pepper, garlic, and jalapeño if desired and cook, stirring, until tender, about 6 minutes. Stir in the spinach and cook, stirring, until the leaves are wilted, about 3 minutes. Add the water, squash, rice, scallions, parsley, cumin, salt, and pepper and bring to a simmer. Cover and cook over medium-low heat until the rice and squash are tender, about 20 minutes. Fluff the rice with a fork and let stand, covered, for about 5 minutes before serving.

Makes 6 servings

Per serving:
205 Calories; 5g Protein; 3g Fat;
41g Carbohydrates; 0 Cholesterol;
413mg Sodium; 2g Fiber

Lime-Basted Sweet Corn

Corn is the most popular vegetable in Mexico. Rather than slathering ears of corn with butter, Mexicans prefer to rub lime over the kernels and sprinkle the corn with chili powder.

6 to 8 ears of corn, shucked
2 limes, quartered
1 to 2 teaspoons chili powder

Bring a large pot of water to a boil. Place the ears of corn in boiling water to cover and cook over medium-high heat until the corn is tender (not mushy), 5 to 7 minutes. (It is important that the water is boiling when you add the corn.) Drain the corn in a large colander and let cool slightly.

Rub the wedges of lime over each ear of corn and sprinkle with chili powder to taste. Serve at once.

Makes 6 to 8 servings

Per serving:
62 Calories; 1g Protein; 0.4g Fat; 13g Carbohydrates; 0 Cholesterol; 7mg Sodium; 4g Fiber

Refried Pinto Beans

Refried comes from the term refritos, *which loosely means "well cooked."*
(It's not a double dose of frying, as the name implies.) This homemade
version is easy to make and lighter tasting than many commercial brands.

**Two 15-ounce cans pinto beans,
  undrained**
1 tablespoon canola oil
1 medium yellow onion, diced
2 large cloves garlic, minced
**1 tablespoon chopped pickled
  jalapeños (optional)**
1 tablespoon dried oregano
½ teaspoon salt
**½ teaspoon freshly ground
  black pepper**

 14oz tomatoes

Drain the canned beans, reserving
½ cup of the liquid.

In a medium saucepan, heat the
oil over medium-high heat. Add
the onion and garlic and cook,
stirring, until tender, about
4 minutes. Add the beans, bean
liquid, jalapeños if desired,
oregano, salt, and pepper. Reduce
heat to medium-low, and cook,
stirring, until beans are thoroughly heated, about 8 minutes.

Transfer the beans to a blender
and process until smooth, leaving
some beans whole, stopping to
stir the beans at least once. Return
the beans to the pan and cook,
over low heat, stirring, about
5 minutes.

Serve the beans as a side dish
or filling for burritos and quesadillas or as a topping for tostadas.

**Makes 3 cups
(6 servings)**

Per serving:
123 Calories, 6g Protein; 3g Fat;
20g Carbohydrates; 0 Cholesterol;
694mg Sodium; 5g Fiber

Squash Picante Pilaf

Mexican chili peppers give this nourishing pilaf a piquant flavor.

1 tablespoon canola oil
1 medium yellow onion, diced
2 cloves garlic, minced
1 to 2 jalapeño or serrano
** peppers, seeded and**
** minced**
3 cups water
2 cups peeled and diced butter-
** nut squash or other winter**
** squash**
1½ cups long-grain white rice
1 cup canned red kidney beans
½ teaspoon salt
½ teaspoon freshly ground
** black pepper**
¼ teaspoon turmeric
3 to 4 tablespoons chopped
** fresh parsley**
2 tablespoons chopped cilantro
** (optional)**

In a medium saucepan, heat the oil over medium heat. Add the onion, garlic, and chili pepper(s) and cook, stirring, until the onions are translucent, about 4 minutes. Stir in the water, squash, rice, beans, salt, pepper, and turmeric and bring to a simmer. Cover the pan and cook over medium-low heat until all of the liquid is absorbed, 15 to 20 minutes.

Fluff the rice with a fork and stir in the parsley, and if desired, cilantro. Let stand, covered, for 5 to 10 minutes before serving.

Makes 4 servings

Per serving:
374 Calories; 9g Protein; 4g Fat;
74g Carbohydrates; 0 Cholesterol;
530mg Sodium; 7g Fiber

Arroz Amarillo
YUCATÁN YELLOW RICE

For this regional favorite, sizzling habanero peppers are simmered with the rice and removed at the finish. This way the chili's heat is subtle, not overwhelming.

1 tablespoon canola oil
1 medium yellow onion, diced
1 red bell pepper, seeded and diced
2 cloves garlic, minced
3 cups water
1½ cups white rice or basmati rice
1 habanero pepper, pierced with a fork
½ teaspoon turmeric
½ teaspoon salt
½ teaspoon freshly ground black pepper

In a medium saucepan, heat the oil over medium heat. Add the onion, bell pepper, and garlic and cook, stirring, until the onion is translucent, about 5 minutes. Stir in the water, rice, habanero, and seasonings and bring to a simmer. Cover and cook over medium-low heat until all of the liquid is absorbed, 15 to 20 minutes.

Remove from the heat and fluff the rice with a fork. Remove the habanero before serving. If desired, slice the habanero into strips and serve to hot-and-spicy aficionados.

Makes 4 servings

Per serving:
282 Calories; 5g Protein; 4g Fat;
56g Carbohydrates; 0 Cholesterol;
277mg Sodium; 2g Fiber

CHAPTER 5

Desserts

Horchata

This soothing rice beverage is enjoyed throughout Mexico and Central America. Typically milk and rice are allowed to steep for several hours before serving, but the widespread availability of rice milk has sped up the process.

4 cups rice milk (see Helpful Hints)
2 cups cooked white or brown rice (see Helpful Hint, page 76)
¼ cup honey
½ teaspoon ground cinnamon

Combine the rice milk, rice, honey, and cinnamon in a blender or a food processor fitted with a steel blade and process until the mixture is smooth (like a milk shake), about 10 seconds. Pour the liquid through a fine sieve, reserving the sweetened liquid. Serve over ice. *¡Salud!*

Makes 4 servings (6 cups)

Helpful Hint

Rice milk is a good beverage to serve with spicy dishes—it cools off the palate.

Per serving:
175 Calories; 9g Protein; 0g Fat; 35g Carbohydrates; 0 Cholesterol; 127mg Sodium; 0g Fiber

Pumpkin-Rum Rice Pudding

Canned pumpkin brings a taste of autumn to this savory rice pudding treat.

**4 cups cooked white or brown
rice (see Helpful Hints,
page 57)**
**1½ cups low-fat milk or soy
milk**
½ cup brown sugar
¼ cup raisins
2 tablespoons dark rum
¼ teaspoon ground cinnamon
¼ teaspoon ground nutmeg
**¼ cup chopped walnuts
(optional)**

In a medium saucepan, combine
the rice, milk, sugar, raisins, rum,
cinnamon, and nutmeg. Cook over
medium-low heat, stirring, until
thickened, 10 to 12 minutes.
Remove from the heat and let cool
slightly. Chill for 30 minutes to
1 hour before serving.

When ready to serve, spoon the
pudding into small bowls. If
desired, sprinkle the walnuts over
the top.

**Makes 6 servings
(about 6 cups)**

Per serving:
260 Calories; 5g Protein; 1g Fat;
55g Carbohydrates; 2mg Cholesterol; 40mg Sodium; 1g Fiber

Chayote Carrot Muffins

Like zucchini, chayote can be used in both savory and sweet dishes.

½ cup store-bought orange juice

½ cup canola oil

⅓ cup white or brown sugar

1 large egg plus 2 large egg whites

2 cups seeded, shredded chayote (see Helpful Hints, page 57)

1 cup peeled and grated carrots

2 cups unbleached all-purpose flour

2 teaspoons baking soda

1 teaspoon baking powder

1 teaspoon salt

1 teaspoon ground cinnamon

1 teaspoon ground nutmeg

1 cup chopped walnuts (optional)

Preheat the oven to 350°F.

In a mixing bowl, whisk together the orange juice, oil, and sugar. Add the egg and egg whites and whisk until the batter is light and creamy. Fold in the remaining ingredients and blend well, form-ing a batter. Pour the batter into lightly greased medium-size muffin tins and place in the oven. Bake until a toothpick inserted in the center comes out clean, 20 to 25 minutes. Remove from the oven and let cool for a few minutes before serving.

Makes 10 to 12 servings (10 to 12 muffins)

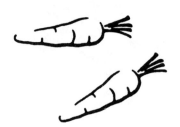

Per serving:
144 Calories; 2g Protein; 11g Fat; 9g Carbohydrates; 21mg Cholesterol; 544mg Sodium; 0g Fiber.

Mixed Fruit Quesadilla

*The versatile tortilla is used to wrap a medley of
fruit in this creative and healthful dessert.*

¼ cup apple juice
1 tablespoon brown sugar
1 large peach or nectarine,
   sliced
1 kiwifruit, peeled and sliced
2 bananas, sliced crosswise
10 to 12 strawberries, hulled
   and sliced
¼ teaspoon ground nutmeg or
   cinnamon
½ cup low-fat plain yogurt
Four 6-inch flour tortillas

In a large skillet, combine the
apple juice and brown sugar. Cook
over medium-high heat, stirring,
until simmering, about 2 minutes.
Add the peach and kiwi and cook,
stirring, until fruit begins to
soften, about 3 minutes. Add the
bananas, strawberries, and
nutmeg and cook, stirring, 3 to
4 minutes.

Meanwhile, warm the tortillas
over a hot burner or in a skillet
and place on serving plates. Spoon
the fruit mixture onto one-half of
each tortilla and top with 2
tablespoons of yogurt. Fold the
tortillas over the filling and serve
at once.

**Makes 4 servings
(4 quesadillas)**

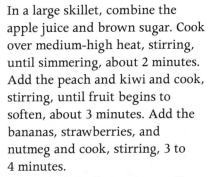

VARIATIONS

*When it's in season, add 2 table-
spoons chopped mint to the fruit
mixture. Other fruits, such
as blueberries, raspberries, or
mangoes, can also be included.*

Per serving:
255 Calories; 7g Protein; 2g Fat;
55g Carbohydrates; 5mg Cholesterol; 239mg Sodium; 9g Fiber

Citrus Flan

Flan is the national dessert of Mexico. A combination of skim milk, egg whites, and reduced-fat condensed milk help to make this traditionally rich custard a tad lighter in calories. It takes a little longer than 30 minutes from start to finish, but most of that is baking time.

2 large eggs
2 large egg whites
1¼ cups skim milk
One 14-ounce can sweetened
　low-fat condensed milk
Juice of 2 limes
Zest of 1 orange (about
　1 tablespoon)

Preheat the oven to 350°F.

In a large mixing bowl, whisk together the eggs and egg whites. Beat in the remaining ingredients. Pour the mixture into eight small ramekins, filling each about three-quarters full. Set the ramekins into a large roasting pan. Fill the pan with hot water until it rises halfway up the sides of the ramekins. Place the pan in the oven and bake until the flans puff up slightly and are firm when gently jiggled, 35 to 45 minutes.

Remove from the oven and cool to room temperature. Refrigerate until chilled, about 2 hours. Serve cold.

**Makes 8 servings
(8 flans)**

Per serving:
117 Calories; 6g Protein; 3g Fat;
16g Carbohydrates; 62mg Cholesterol; 81mg Sodium; 0g Fiber

Tropical Fruit Flambé

Tropical fruits grow abundantly in Mexico. For this flashy dessert, mangoes and bananas are flambéed in a fruity rum sauce.

¼ cup apple juice
2 tablespoons brown sugar
1 large ripe mango, peeled, pitted, and sliced
3 to 4 bananas, peeled and sliced crosswise
¼ teaspoon ground cinnamon
¼ cup dark rum
Splash of banana liqueur (optional)
4 cups low-fat vanilla frozen yogurt

Helpful Hint

When flambéing, never pour liquor directly from the bottle to the pan. Always measure out the liquor into a small pitcher and pour it from the pitcher.

In a large skillet, combine the apple juice and brown sugar. Cook over medium heat, stirring, until simmering, 3 to 4 minutes. Add the mango, bananas, and cinnamon and cook for 3 to 4 minutes, turning the fruit and gently coating with the juice-and-sugar mixture.

Remove the pan from the heat and add the rum and liqueur if desired. Return to the heat and bring to a simmer. Carefully touch a lighted match to the pan, flambéing the fruit mixture. Allow the flame to subside and continue cooking for 1 minute.

Scoop the low-fat frozen yogurt into serving bowls and spoon the fruit over the top.

Makes 4 servings

Per serving:
418 Calories; 9g Protein; 3g Fat; 85g Carbohydrates; 10mg Cholesterol; 85mg Sodium; 3g Fiber

Mexican Hot Chocolate

Cocoa beans, along with corn, squash, and tomatoes, are indigenous to Mexico. Cinnamon-flavored hot chocolate drinks have been enjoyed for centuries. (This beverage puts to shame that package of hot cocoa mix sitting in the back of the cupboard.)

2 cups skim milk or soy milk
2 to 3 ounces semisweet baking chocolate
1 tablespoon honey
½ teaspoon ground cinnamon

In a sturdy saucepan, gently cook all of the ingredients over medium-low heat until the chocolate is melted, stirring frequently with a whisk, about 7 minutes. (Don't let the milk boil.) Then vigorously whisk the mixture until it is slightly frothy.

When it is steaming hot and frothy, pour into large cups or mugs. Serve at once.

**Makes 2 servings
(2 cups)**

VARIATIONS

Adding a dash of almond extract or coffee liqueur is a fun way to spice up the beverage.

Per serving:
249 Calories; 10g Protein; 9g Fat; 38g Carbohydrates; 4mg Cholesterol; 126mg Sodium; 2g Fiber

Strawberry Margarita Sorbet

The ultimate Mexican party drink is the obvious inspiration for this chilled fruit dessert. Whip this up the day before serving to give it time to freeze.

1 cup apple juice
1 cup water
½ cup sugar
2 pints fresh strawberries,
**   hulled and diced (about**
**   4 cups)**
2 tablespoons Triple Sec
2 tablespoons tequila
Juice of 1 lime
1 lime, thinly sliced

In a medium saucepan, combine the apple juice, water, and sugar and bring to a simmer. Cook over medium heat for about 10 minutes, stirring occasionally. Add the strawberries, Triple Sec, tequila, and lime juice and set aside for 5 minutes.

Add the strawberry mixture to a blender or food processor fitted with a steel blade and process until liquefied, about 10 seconds. Transfer to a plastic container with a lid and freeze for 2 to 4 hours or overnight. Stir the sorbet once or twice after 1 hour.

To serve, scoop the sorbet into small serving bowls and garnish with the lime slices.

Makes eight ¾-cup servings

Per serving:
84 Calories; 0g Protein; 0g Fat;
19g Carbohydrates; 0 Cholesterol;
1mg Sodium; 0g Fiber

Pineapple-Apricot Rice Pudding

*Pineapple and apricots add a fruity nuance
to this light version of rice pudding.*

**3 cups cooked rice (see Helpful
   Hint, page 36)**
**1½ cups low-fat milk or soy
   milk**
**One 15-ounce can diced pine-
   apple or pineapple chunks
   with liquid**
1 cup chopped dried apricots
½ cup brown or white sugar
¼ cup raisins
**2 to 3 tablespoons grated
   sweetened coconut
   (optional)**
¼ teaspoon ground cinnamon

In a medium saucepan, combine
rice, milk, pineapple and its
liquid, apricots, sugar, raisins, and
coconut if desired. Cook, stirring,
10 to 12 minutes. Remove from the
heat and let cool slightly. Chill for
30 minutes to 1 hour before
serving.

When ready to serve, spoon the
pudding into bowls and sprinkle
with cinnamon.

Makes 6 servings

Per serving:
316 Calories; 5g Protein; 1g Fat;
74g Carbohydrates; 2mg Cholesterol; 42mg Sodium; 1g Fiber

Banana-Strawberry Tostada Sundae

Here is a fruity Mexican twist on an ice cream sundae, minus the ice cream.
(Tostadas replace the waffle cone and yogurt replaces the ice cream.)

4 tostada shells
½ cup apple juice
1 tablespoon dark rum
   (optional)
1 tablespoon brown sugar
3 bananas, peeled and cut into
   ½-inch slices
6 to 8 strawberries, hulled and
   sliced
¼ teaspoon ground cinnamon
1 pint nonfat vanilla or choco-
   late frozen yogurt
¼ cup unsalted roasted peanuts

Preheat the oven to 350°F.

Arrange the tostada shells on a large baking pan. Place in the oven and bake for 4 to 6 minutes. Remove from the oven and arrange on a large serving platter.

In a large skillet, mix together the apple juice, rum if desired, and brown sugar. Cook, stirring, over medium heat until simmering, about 2 minutes. Add the bananas, strawberries, and cinnamon and cook, stirring occasionally, until the fruit is soft but not mushy, about 3 minutes. Remove the skillet from the heat.

With an ice cream scooper, spoon the frozen yogurt over each tostada. Spoon the bananas and strawberries over the yogurt. Sprinkle each with the peanuts. The tostadas can either be eaten by hand or off a plate. Either way, don't forget the napkins.

Makes 4 servings
(4 sundaes)

VARIATIONS

Other sundae toppings can include hot chocolate syrup, pistachio nuts, mango slices, and/or diced pineapple.

Helpful Hint

Mexican Hot Chocolate (page 154) is an ideal beverage to serve with this.

Per serving:
317 Calories; 8g Protein; 7g Fat; 57g Carbohydrates; 18mg Cholesterol; 79mg Sodium; 3g Fiber

Capriotada

MEXICAN BREAD PUDDING

*Unlike American bread desserts, this Mexican version relies on low-fat
cheese instead of eggs, cream, or butter. You'll be amazed how dried-out
bread is transformed into a scrumptious dessert.*

**1 medium loaf French bread,
cut into cubes (about
8 ounces), see Helpful Hint**
1½ cups apple juice
1½ cups water
1 cup brown sugar
½ cup raisins
2 tablespoons honey
1 teaspoon ground cinnamon
**1 cup shredded low-fat
Monterey Jack cheese**
½ cup diced walnuts
**1 pint nonfat frozen yogurt (any
flavor)**

Preheat the oven to 300°F.

Arrange the bread cubes on a
baking pan and place in the oven.
Bake until the bread is dry but not
toasted, 8 to 10 minutes, stirring
the cubes once or twice. Remove
from the heat and toss into a
medium mixing bowl.

Meanwhile, in a medium
saucepan, combine the juice,
water, sugar, raisins, honey, and
cinnamon and bring to a simmer.
Cook over medium-low heat until
the mixture is syrupy, about
15 minutes, stirring frequently.
Set aside to cool for 5 minutes.

Turn the oven up to 375°F. Add
the cheese and nuts to the bread
cubes and toss together. Pour the
syrup over the bread mixture and
let stand to absorb the syrup for
2 or 3 minutes. Spoon into an
8-inch square baking pan and
bake until firm in the center,
about 15 minutes.

Serve the bread pudding in
bowls along side scoops of frozen
yogurt.

**Makes 6 to 8 servings
(6 to 8 cups)**

Helpful Hint

*This is the perfect opportunity
to use stale bread.*

Per 1-cup serving:
495 Calories; 9g Protein; 10g Fat;
89g Carbohydrates; 16mg Cholesterol; 332mg Sodium; 2g Fiber

Tropical Ambrosia

Here's a healthy Mexican twist on the classic fruit salad.

**One 20-ounce can pineapple
  chunks, drained**
**One 11-ounce can mandarin
  orange segments, drained**
**1 large ripe mango, peeled,
  pitted, and diced**
1 banana, peeled and diced
8 ounces low-fat plain yogurt
1 to 2 tablespoons honey
¼ teaspoon ground cinnamon

Combine all of the ingredients in
a medium mixing bowl and blend
together. Chill the salad for 15
minutes before serving.

Makes 4 servings

VARIATIONS

*If mangoes are unavailable,
substitute one 17-ounce can apricot
halves, diced. Other seasonal fruits,
such as seedless grapes, sweet
cherries, blueberries, or strawberries, can also be added.*

Per serving:
190 Calories; 5g Protein; 1g Fat;
43g Carbohydrates; 3mg Cholesterol; 43amg Sodium; 3g Fiber

Pineapple Mango Crisp

One 20-ounce can pineapple chunks, drained

2 ripe mangoes, peeled, pitted, and coarsely chopped

2 tablespoons honey

Juice of 1 lime

½ teaspoon ground nutmeg

1 cup rolled oats (the old-fashioned style)

¾ cup all-purpose flour

½ cup brown sugar

½ teaspoon ground cinnamon

3 to 4 tablespoons margarine, softened

1 pint low-fat vanilla frozen yogurt (optional)

Preheat the oven to 375°F.

In a mixing bowl, combine the pineapple, mangoes, honey, lime juice, and nutmeg. Spread the fruit mixture over the bottom of an 8-inch square greased baking dish.

Meanwhile, combine the oats, flour, brown sugar, and cinnamon in a large mixing bowl. With a fork or pastry cutter, cut the margarine into the dry ingredients until the mixture is crumbly. Sprinkle the topping evenly over the fruit. Bake until the topping is lightly browned, about 20 minutes.

If desired, serve the fruit crisp with a scoop of frozen yogurt spooned over the top.

Makes 6 servings

Per serving:
417 Calories; 7g Protein; 8g Fat; 79g Carbohydrates; 7mg Cholesterol; 108mg Sodium; 4g Fiber

Mango Rice Pudding

A delicious coral-hued mango gives this rice pudding a tropical personality.

3 cups cooked white or brown rice (see Helpful Hint, page 36)
1½ cups low-fat milk or soy milk
1 ripe mango, peeled, pitted, and diced
½ cup brown or white sugar
¼ cup raisins
½ teaspoon ground nutmeg

In a medium saucepan, combine rice, milk, mango, sugar, and raisins. Cook, stirring, 10 to 12 minutes. Remove from the heat and let cool slightly. Chill for 30 minutes to 1 hour before serving.

When ready to serve, spoon the pudding into bowls and sprinkle with nutmeg.

Makes 6 servings

Per serving:
237 Calories; 5g Protein; 1g Fat; 54g Carbohydrates; 2mg Cholesterol; 40mg Sodium; 1g Fiber

Index